O9-AIE-136

10-Minute
Home Repairs

10-Minute
Home Repairs

More Than 200 Fast, Effective Fixes You Can Do Yourself

JERRI FARRIS

FAIR WINDS
PRESS
GLOUCESTER, MASSACHUSETTS

Text © 2006 by Fair Winds Press

First published in the USA in 2006 by
Fair Winds Press, a member of
Quayside Publishing Group
33 Commercial Street
Gloucester, MA 01930

All rights reserved. No part of this book may be reproduced or utilized, in any
form or by any means, electronic or mechanical, without prior permission in
writing from the publisher.

10 09 08 07 06   1 2 3 4 5

ISBN 1-59233-203-X

Library of Congress Cataloging-in-Publication Data
Farris, Jerri.
  10-minute home repairs : more than 200 fast, effective fixes you can
do yourself / Jerri Farris.
    p. cm.
  ISBN 1-59233-203-X (pbk.)
  1. Dwellings--Maintenance and repair--Amateurs' manuals. 2.
Do-it-yourself work. I. Title: Ten minute home repairs. II. Title.
  TH4817.3.F375 2006
  643'.7--dc22

                                    2005028617

Book design by Anne Gram
Cover illustration by Elizabeth Cornaro
Illustrations by Robert Leanna
Printed and bound in USA

To my dad,

Chuck Farris,

and my mom,

Nora Farris,

who taught me to rise to the occasion.

Notice to Reader:

Use caution, care, and good judgment when following the procedures described in this book. The publisher cannot assume responsibility for any damage to property or injury to persons as a result of misuse of the information provided. Always follow manufacturers' instructions included with products and materials.

Table of Contents

Chapter 1

Ready, Set, Repair!

Almost every homeowner in the world has a list—either written on paper or floating at the back of his or her mind—of small repairs that need to be done around the house. Most homeowners are waiting for the right time, the right materials, or the right information to come along so they can get started on these projects. Well, now that you're armed with the information in *10-Minute Home Repairs*, that time is now!

Make Time

If you think you're too busy to get your home in better shape, think again. You can fix that annoying faucet leak or the creaky floor board that's bugged you for months in the time it takes to boil a pot of pasta! Read through this book, and see for yourself. It's filled with easy projects, almost all of which can be done in ten minutes or less. Think of how accomplished you'll feel when you fit a successful home repair into your day!

Develop a Can-Do Attitude

No matter how much experience you have (or don't have) around the house, you can do every project in this book. How can I be so sure? I can do every one, and I once was the most inexperienced, timid homeowner ever to pick up a screwdriver.

I grew up the least handy person in an extremely handy family, and I married an extremely handy man. My version of fixing something was to point out the problem and wait. Then one day, I suddenly and unexpectedly found myself in charge of a big suburban house and yard. To say I was intimidated by this responsibility is like saying water is wet. But, necessity being the mother of invention and all, I tried. I read books, called my dad and mom thousands of times, and turned to friends and neighbors for advice and guidance. And I learned. I did just about everything wrong at least once, but I learned. In fact, I learned so much that I've been writing books on home repair and home décor for more than a decade now, and I love it.

Take a Ten-Minute Tour

If home maintenance is new to you, familiarize yourself with your house and its systems. Go on a ten-minute tour of all the rooms in your home. If you come across things you don't understand or things that look like problems, consult friends with more experience or call on experts. Preventive maintenance is virtually always less expensive than emergency repairs.

Sweat the Small Stuff

Small-scale ten-minute repairs are worth every minute of your time. In fact, they can help reduce the need for bigger, more complicated repairs. Here is a true story: A soap dish fell off the shower wall in my friend's home. Everyone ignored the problem and went on with their busy lives. Every time someone took a shower, water ran down the hole, behind the tile, and into the framing. It took several months, but eventually the shower wall collapsed. By the time my friend got around to assessing the situation, the waterlogged wood had started to rot and—not only the walls but the floor, too—had to be replaced.

Take care of small problems while they're still small, and they take only a few minutes. Ignore them, and they grow—sometimes into large, expensive projects. It would have cost less than $25 to replace the soap dish when it first fell off, but my friend ended up spending thousands of dollars to fix the water damage caused by its absence.

Easy Organizing

Keeping good records of all things related to your home and
   home repairs will save you lots of time, stress, and money in
   the long run. You may come up with a better system, but here is
   one that works for me: Get a large three-ring binder and divide
   it into the following four clearly labeled sections.

Section 1: Fixture or appliance receipts. This gives you the
   necessary information—date and place of purchase, model
   number, and so on—to order parts later on or take advan-
   tage of warranties.

Section 2: Repair receipts. This gives you a paper trail of the
   repairs done to the house and reminds you who did the repairs.
   If anything goes wrong, you know who to hold accountable, and
   if everything goes right, you know who to call on next time.

Section 3: Owner's manuals for all appliances, fixtures, and tools.

Section 4 (my favorite section): Notes on the colors, numbers, and
  manufacturers of the paint, wallpaper, and flooring in the
  house. The manufacturer no longer offers the color of the paint
  on my door moldings and trim, but my favorite paint store can
  still mix up a batch, because I have the original formula.
  Records like this will serve you well, over and over again.

Tools of the Trade
TOOL KIT ESSENTIALS

Although it's easy to spend a lot of money on tools, it's not necessary. Get a five-gallon bucket and a fabric tool organizer that fits inside it, and begin building a basic tool kit. The tools below are the essentials you'll need to perform most ten-minute home repairs. They appear in roughly the order of their importance to common repairs.

- Claw hammer
- Flat-head screwdriver
- Phillips screwdriver
- Tape measure
- Adjustable wrench
- Set of pliers, including slip-joint, needle nose, and locking pliers
- Utility knife
- Putty and broad knives
- Cordless drill and bit set
- Level, standard or laser
- Quick clamps
- Stud finder

Over time, you'll discover how much easier it is to do a job with the right tool than one that's almost right, and your tool kit will expand to fill the space and budget you have available for it.

Quick Tip When tool lust hits, try to keep your wits about you. It might be better to share unusual or expensive tools, like a power washer, with neighbors, family, or friends.

HELPFUL SUPPLIES

All good intentions aside, virtually no project can be done in ten minutes if you have to go to the store first. Keeping common materials on hand makes it easy to do projects in a few spare minutes. The following items prove very useful:

- Wood screws
- Drywall screws
- Sheet-metal screws
- Hollow-wall anchors
- Finish nails
- Box nails
- Wood glue
- Polyurethane glue (such as Gorilla Glue)
- Silicone caulk
- Ultra-light spackle
- Wood filler
- Sandpaper and sanding sponges
- Painter's tape
- Silicon spray or spray lubricant

Safety Alert

Safety cannot be emphasized enough when it comes to home repair. Some common repair materials are toxic, others are flammable; live wires are dangerous, and some gases are explosive. Use your own common sense in addition to the rules listed here.

Live Wires

First and foremost, *never* work on live wires. Turn off the power, and test the receptacle before you begin any electrical project (see pages 199 to 201).

Ventilation

When a product label tells you to use "adequate ventilation," it means that there should be no more fumes in the room than there would be if you were using the product outdoors. Open windows, set up a fan to draw dust and fumes out of the room, turn on exhaust fans—whatever it takes to provide fresh air to the area. If you're not sure the ventilation is adequate, wear a respirator while you work.

Lighting

You might not think that good lighting and safety go together like nacho chips and cheese, but they do. It's easy to make mistakes when you can't see clearly. A bright light on a flexible hose or spring clamp lets you see all the parts you should and shouldn't touch!

Equipment

Finally, safety equipment: disposable gloves, work gloves, heavy boots, safety glasses, hearing protection, and particle masks are essential for home repairs. Buy them and use them.

Chapter 2

Good Boundaries

Walls, floors, and ceilings are the largest surfaces in the house and have a direct impact on the impression the interior makes on those who visit. Here are some quick ways to make a great impression.

Walls
DIRT AND GRIME

Spot clean painted walls. Dampen a soft rag with white vinegar and carefully wash the spot. Scrub gently—you don't want to damage the paint.

Quick Tip If you don't already have Mr. Clean Magic Erasers in your cleaning caddy, get thyself to a grocery store and buy some. When I discovered these things, you'd have thought I'd found gold in the backyard. Dampen one with plain water, and gently wipe away dirt, grime, and scuff marks.

> **Quick Tip** To clean greasy kitchen walls, combine one cup of ammonia, 1 cup of white vinegar, and 1/4 cup of dishwashing liquid with 1 gallon of warm water. Test in an inconspicuous area.

Vacuum wallpapered walls.

Vacuum wallpapered walls with a long brush attachment and a gentle touch. Clean the brush itself before you start, especially if the wallpaper is flocked or textured.

Wash wallpapered walls.

Wallpapers labeled *washable* can be gently washed with a mild cleaning solution and a rag or sponge. Wallpapers labeled *scrubable* can be washed as though they were painted.

Remove mold from walls.

Mold and mildew are unhealthy for you *and* your house. Combine 1/4 cup of chlorine bleach and 1 gallon of plain water. (Never mix chlorine with other cleaning chemicals.) Wear rubber gloves, and make sure you have plenty of fresh air while you work: Open a window or run a vent fan. Make sure everyone in the family uses the vent fan every time they shower or bathe. If the mold or mildew still returns repeatedly, call a mold abatement specialist.

DENTS AND GAPS

Secure popped drywall nails.

As a house settles, nails often pop to the surface of the walls. Hammering them down is just a temporary fix. Instead, drive a drywall screw into a stud a couple of inches away from the popped nail, and then hammer the nail below the surface. Fill both holes with ultra-light spackle, sand the area, and touch up the paint.

Fill cracked drywall seams.

In a new house, it's normal for small cracks to develop at seams and joints. New, nylon drywall tape is the key to a permanent solution. Use a taping knife to fill the cracked seam with joint compound. Smooth a piece of drywall tape over the crack, working from the center toward the edges. Cover the tape with a thin layer of compound, and let it dry. Apply a second coat, feathering the edges. Sand, prime, and repaint the area.

> **Quick Tip** Spread spackle or joint compound on a wall repair so it's thinner on the edges than it is in the middle. This technique, known as feathering the edges, blends the repair into the surrounding area more easily.

Retape cracked joints between walls and ceilings.

First, use a taping knife to cut through the existing tape, then apply nylon seam tape and compound as you would for a seam (see page 27).

Camouflage dents or shallow holes in drywall.

Scrape the area smooth using a putty knife. Next, smooth ultra-light spackle into the hole. Ultra-light spackle dries in just a few minutes, so by the time you get the knife washed up, you should be ready to sand and repaint the area.

Patch large holes in drywall. Cut away the damaged area, leaving a neat square or rectangle. Cut a patch to fit and two strips of drywall, each strip two inches larger than the hole. Use hot glue to attach the strips to the back of the drywall at the top and bottom of the hole. When the glue is cool, put a bead of hot glue on the front of each backer strip and press the patch into place. Let the glue cool for a few minutes, then apply nylon drywall tape and joint compound. Add a second coat of compound and feather the edges. Sand, prime, and paint the area.

Quick Tip To remove nails without damaging the walls, put a small block of wood between the head of the hammer and the wall before you begin to pry.

Patch deep holes in drywall.

If the edges of the hole are cracked, or the hole goes all the way through the drywall, buy a peel-and-stick repair patch. Press the patch in place, and cover it with spackle or joint compound. When the spackle is thoroughly dry, add a second coat. Let the second coat dry, then sand, prime, and repaint the area.

Quick Tip Placing sturdy door stops behind every door can keep them from opening so wide that they cause damage to your walls.

Fasten loose wallpaper seams.

Buy wallpaper adhesive and a special adhesive syringe at a paint store or home center. Squirt some adhesive under both edges of the seam, and press them into place. If the paper isn't flocked or embossed, roll the area with a seam roller. (If you don't have a seam roller, use a small rolling pin.) Wipe away excess adhesive with a damp sponge.

Remove wallpaper bubbles.

When wallpaper glue stops sticking, bubbles pop up. To deflate a bubble, cut a slit through it with a utility knife. Squirt wallpaper adhesive onto the wall under it, and press the paper into place. Wipe away excess adhesive with a damp sponge.

Fix a damaged section of wallpaper.

Tape a scrap of wallpaper over the damaged area, lining up the pattern exactly. (Painter's tape works well, because it releases easily.) With a utility knife, cut around the damaged area, pressing hard enough to cut through both layers of the paper. Peel up the patch and remove the damaged section. Spread adhesive on the back of the new patch, align the pattern carefully, and press it into place. Wipe away excess adhesive with a damp sponge.

Quick Tip Put a new blade in your utility knife before cutting wallpaper.

SHELVES AND WALL HANGINGS

Hang a picture.

Measure from the top of the frame to the hanging hardware and from the sides of the frame to the hardware. Next, lightly mark the wall where you want the top of the picture to sit. If you're using a standard level, draw a level line on the wall, lower than the original mark by the distance from the top of the frame to the hardware. With the laser level, shoot a line at that position. Mark screw holes to match the hanging hardware and drill pilot holes. If you hit a stud (you'll feel the resistance), drive wood screws into the pilot holes. If not, drive self-tapping wall anchors into the holes, and then drive screws into the anchors.

Quick Tip Interior decorators say the center of a picture should be at eye level. If you're hanging a collection of framed pieces, the center of the collection should be roughly at eye level.

Quick Tip To support the weight of a picture or mirror up to 150 pounds, use a special wire wall hanger. These simple, inexpensive gizmos can be purchased at home and garden shows or ordered online (check out www.heavydutywallhanger.com). Just twist the end of this hook-shaped hanger into the drywall, and push the wire up and into place.

Hang a shelf.

Most shelves come with brackets—at least two, but possibly more, depending on their length. On the back of each bracket, you'll find hanging hardware. Hold the shelf and a bracket together as though they were on the wall, and measure the distance from the top of the shelf to the center of the first screw hole. Next, measure the distance between the screw holes on the bracket, center to center. Write these measurements down. Next, draw a level line where you want the top of the shelf. Now it's time to use the first measurement: Shoot (with a laser level) or draw (with a spirit level) a line lower than the original mark by that distance. Mark and drill pilot holes for the top screw on each bracket. Shoot or draw a level line for the second set of screws, and then mark and drill pilot holes for them. If you feel the drill bit hit a stud, use wood screws. If not, drive self-tapping wall anchors into the holes and then drive screws into the anchors. Hang the brackets from the screws, and then position the shelf on top of them.

Quick Tip Murphy's Law: If you strip a screw (wreck its slots when you drive it), you'll probably need to remove it with a screw extractor. The exact instructions vary a little depending on the manufacturer, but basically you put the extractor bit into your drill, and drive it into the stripped screw, creating threads for the extractor to grip. Next, you reverse the drill and back the screw out of its hole. A screw extractor isn't very expensive, but it's worth its weight in gold.

PAINTING WALLS

Okay, I admit that painting a wall the right way takes longer than ten minutes. To make this project less overwhelming, it's been broken up into smaller ten-minute tasks on prepping walls, painting techniques, preparing equipment, and cleaning up right.

When it comes to painting, the three most important tasks are preparation, preparation, and preparation—so let's start there. After all, a coat of paint isn't going to cover dents, cracks, or ridges in the joint compound.

Scrape off any cracked or peeling paint.

Don't paint over peeling paint—in no time flat, the new paint will peel, too, and you'll be right back where you started. Use a putty knife to scrape away all the loose paint, then fill the chipped area with a thin coat of ultra-light spackle. Feather the edges of the spackle so you can't see the patch. When the spackle is dry, sand it with fine sandpaper until you can't feel the edges. Now it's ready for priming and painting.

Quick Tip Fine sandpaper carries a label of at least 150-grit. "Grit" refers to the number of grainy particles found per inch of paper; the higher the grit number, the smoother the paper, and conversely the lower the grit number the rougher the paper.

Fill any holes.

Use a putty knife to smooth ultra-light spackle into any small holes. If there are larger holes, cracked seams, or popped drywall nails, repair them before you paint (see page 27).

Quick Tip Here's an idea that's good for your budget and for the planet: buy recycled paint. It costs about 50 percent less than regular paint, and keeps unused paint out of the waste stream. Local recycling program officials can direct you to authorized dealers in your area. They also can tell you how to donate unused paint.

Test paint for lead.

Lead, a common additive in paint manufactured before 1978, poses serious health hazards, especially for children. Adding lead to paint was outlawed in 1978, so if your house was built before that time, you need to test the paint for lead before you sand, scrape, or repair any painted walls or wood in your house. You can get an inexpensive test kit at any paint store, hardware store, or home center. If you find lead, get expert help before you sand, scrape, cut into, or paint any painted surface. Most paint stores and home centers offer free brochures on what they call "lead abatement procedures." You also can find useful information at www.epa.gov.

Sand down all lumps, bumps, and ridges.

Turn on a bright light, and check out the walls. If you see bumps or ridges, sand them down with fine-grit sandpaper or a sanding sponge. This may sound like a hassle, but you'll be glad you did it when you see the final result.

Quick Tip When you're painting an entire room, do it in the logical order. Start with the ceiling, then do the trim, windows, and doors, and then the walls. Check the label for the paint's curing time, and allow plenty of time between jobs so you can mask and drape without damaging the work you just finished.

Protect hanging light fixtures.

It only takes a minute to protect any hanging fixture. First, shut off the power to the circuit. Next, remove the screws from the plate cover (the round thing on the ceiling) and slide it down the chain. Finally, pull a large trash bag up from the bottom of the fixture and tie it around the chain.

Protect walls and other surfaces.

To keep paint from accidentally splashing your walls, floors, or other decor, use trash bags or sheet plastic to cover exposed surfaces. This is one of those jobs that can be trickier than it seems, unless you know the trick! Two-inch painter's tape is sturdy enough to hold sheet plastic on the walls. Beware: if you try to put tape on the plastic before hanging it, the weight of the plastic will pull the tape off the wall, and you'll feel like you're wrestling an alligator. The trick is to put the tape on the wall first and—most importantly—to press down only the top half. With the tape in place and the bottom half loose, all you have to do is slide the edge of the sheet plastic under it and press. Presto! That job is done. (It helps to be smarter than the alligator!)

Quick Tip Protect your toilet while painting in the bathroom with a trash bag. It's just the right size to cover a toilet. Drop one over the top, and tape the edges of the bag to the floor. You're good to go.

Protect faceplates and other wall fixtures.

Remove the faceplates from all switches, receptacles, and vent covers. If there's a thermostat on the wall, take it down, or mask it with wide painter's tape.

Protect baseboards, window casings, and door casings with tape.

It's easier to paint the walls if you don't have to worry about dripping or splashing onto the trim. Apply painter's masking tape to all the trim in the room—the baseboards, window casings, and door casings. Line up the edge of the tape with the inside edge of the trim and press.

Quick Tip Run the tip of a putty knife along the inside edge of the tape to keep the paint from leaking underneath the tape.

Dampen roller covers.

A damp roller cover soaks up paint more evenly than a dry one, which makes it easy to roll out an even coat. Before you start painting, dampen the cover using water for latex paint or special solvent designed for alkyd paint. Squeeze out the excess, put the cover on a roller frame, and set the whole thing inside a plastic bag to keep it damp until you're ready to paint. Note: Be very careful with alkyd solvents. The fumes are flammable.

Quick Tip To avoid having to pick fuzzy blobs out of freshly painted walls, remove lint from new roller covers before using them. Wrap masking tape around your hand—sticky side out— and pat the cover. Change the tape when it's no longer sticky, and keep patting until no more lint sticks to the tape.

Mix paint with a drill.

Paint separates quickly, so it's important to stir paint right before using it. The problem is, if the paint's been sitting around too long, it takes a lot of stirring to get the job done right. Instead of a stick, use a paint-mixer bit and a variable-speed drill. It's quick and easy. Two notes of caution: First, put the drill on a low speed—you don't want air bubbles in the paint. Second, keep the head of the bit down in the paint as long as the drill's running so you don't throw paint all over the room. (Yes, this is the voice of experience speaking.)

Quick Tip Even custom-mixed paint can vary a tiny bit from one can to the next. If your project will take more than one can of paint, pour all of it into a large bucket, and mix thoroughly. This technique, called "boxing" the paint, prevents color shifts in the middle of a project.

> **Quick Tip** After you wash a brush, comb its bristles with the spiked side of a roller-cleaning tool. The roller cleaner, an inexpensive tool you can find at most paint stores and home centers, straightens the bristles so the brush dries in the right shape.

Start by "cutting in" with a small brush. Use a small brush, and start at the edges of the wall. This is called "cutting in." Stop after a few feet, and use a roller on the center before the edges dry. If you wait too long to use the roller, you most likely will see a line between the roller paint and the edge work, so try to keep a steady pace. If there are two people painting, one of you can "cut-in" around the edges, while another rolls right behind them. Most walls will need two coats of paint, but brand-new walls and deep paint colors may require three.

Quick Tip Just about everyone who has ever painted has put off cleaning a paintbrush for "just a minute" and returned to find a stiff paintbrush. When this happens to you (and you're using latex paint), pour white vinegar into a glass jar—just enough to cover the bristles of the brush. Heat the vinegar in the microwave. You want the vinegar to be hot but not boiling. Soak the brush in the vinegar for an hour or so, then wash it thoroughly with soap and mild detergent. This trick usually saves the brush.

Dispose of and store paint safely.

Be kind to the planet when you dispose of paint. If there's less than an inch of latex paint left in a can, leave the lid off and let it dry out. Most communities allow small amounts of dried latex paint to be thrown in the regular trash. Alkyd paint always has to be treated as hazardous waste. If there's more than an inch of paint, cover the can with plastic wrap, then replace the lid. Tap the edges of the lid with a rubber mallet to make sure the lid is on securely. Write the date and the name of the room where the paint was used on the lid, then place the can, upside down, in storage. (The paint against the lid keeps air from infiltrating the can. Just make sure the lid's on tight before you turn it upside down.) Don't let the paint freeze, and don't store it near a gas furnace or water heater.

Recycle leftover paint.

If there is more than an inch of latex paint left in a can, it can be recycled. Check with your community's hazardous waste disposal facility—most operate recycling programs. Store the paint as described on page 47, and take it to the collection facility as soon as practical.

Dispose of and store paint thinner.

Pour used paint thinner into a glass jar, and let it stand until the solid material settles to the bottom. Pour off the clear thinner and reuse it. Dispose of the solids as hazardous waste.

> **Quick Tip** Never pour paint thinner down a drain. Everything you pour down a drain becomes part of the water system.

Floors
HARDWOOD FLOORS

Silence squeaky floors by powdering joints between boards.

When the joints between hardwood boards swell, the boards rub against each other and squeak when you walk across them. If you reduce the friction between the boards, the squeak will quiet down. Start by scraping any dirt and gunk out of the joints, and then sprinkle a little baby powder between the squeaky boards. Bounce up and down on the boards to work the powder into the joint. If baby powder doesn't do the trick, try graphite powder.

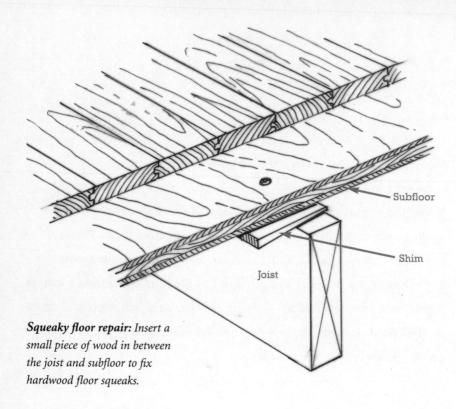

Subfloor

Shim

Joist

Squeaky floor repair: *Insert a small piece of wood in between the joist and subfloor to fix hardwood floor squeaks.*

Stop squeaks by filling gaps between the subfloor and joists.

The part of the floor you see sits on top of a subfloor, typically plywood, that is, in turn, supported by large boards called *joists*. If there aren't enough screws holding the subfloor to the joists or the joists themselves have shrunk, gaps appear and can cause squeaking. You can fill these gaps with hardwood shims, small, tapered pieces of wood that you can buy at a home center. Measure from the squeak or soft spot to the wall or some other landmark so you'll be able to find it from below. When you find the gap, squirt some wood glue into it, and put a little on the end of a shim. Use a hammer to tap the shim into the gap, just until the shim is snug. Stay off the floor until the glue is dry.

Quick Tip Wood shrinks and swells with changes in humidity. If you maintain a humidity level between 35 and 55 percent, your house isn't exposed to damaging seasonal cycles. This means using a dehumidifier in the summer and a humidifier in the winter.

Stop floor squeaks by refastening loose boards. As hardwood expands and contracts along with seasonal changes in temperature and humidity, nails work loose, and the hardwood pulls away from the subfloor. When you step on a loose board, it rides up and down the nail, and you hear a squeak. If you can get to the floor joists from underneath (from an unfinished basement, for example), drill pilot holes, and drive wood screws up through the subfloor and into the hardwood. If you have to work from above, drill pilot holes in the loose boards, and drive ring-shank nails through them into the subfloor. (The nails hold better if you drive them at a slight angle.) Countersink the nails, and fill the holes with tinted wood putty.

> **Quick Tip** There are all different types of hardwood floors. Find out if your floors are solid hardwood, and know what kind of finish they have before you attempt to clean them. No matter what type of wood floor you have, avoid using ammonia or cleaning products that contain ammonia.

Quick Tip If you're driving screws from beneath a subfloor, you'll need to know what length screws to use: too short, and they won't hold; too long, and they'll go through the wood. To determine the right length, find a heat register in the floor. By pulling up the register cover and looking at the exposed edges of the floor, you should be able to measure the layers of flooring. Choose screws that reach all the way through the subfloor and halfway into the hardwood.

Replace furniture wheels with casters and glides.

Some chairs and tables have small wheels that can dent wood floors. Barrel-type casters and wide, flat glides distribute weight over a larger area and prevent dents. Replace small wheels with larger casters and glides, which can be found in hardware stores and home centers.

Quick Tip Leave your spike and stiletto heels at the door. Even on a small-to-average woman, high heels produce dynamic loads of more than 1,000 pounds per square inch—more than enough to create serious dents in resilient or hardwood floors.

Quick Tip According to The Marble Institute of America, it takes at least eight steps to get the dirt off your shoes after you walk into the house. Put rugs and runners at each entrance to protect your floors from dirt and grit.

Get stains out of hardwood.

This is an easy but delicate job. The first step is removing the finish in the area with fine sandpaper. Next, dissolve oxalic acid crystals in water, following the manufacturer's directions. (You can find these crystals at paint retailers, hardware stores, or home centers.) Use a clean cotton rag to blot the solution directly on the discolored area; go do something fun while the solution soaks for an hour. If you can still see the stain an hour later, add more solution. When the discoloration is gone, dissolve two tablespoons of borax into a pint of water, and use the solution to wash the area. Rinse, and let the floor dry. Lightly sand the area, then apply wood restorer to blend it into the surrounding floor.

Fill scratches and dents in hardwood.

Buy a tinted latex wood patching compound. Use a putty knife to press the compound, into the scratch. Scrape away any excess compound and let the patch dry. Sand lightly—with the grain of the wood—until the patch is even with the surrounding wood. Apply several coats of wood restorer.

Carpeted Floors

Fix a squeaky, carpeted floor.

When a carpeted floor squeaks, usually the problem is that the subfloor is rubbing against the joists. If you can get to the floor from beneath, you can fix this by shimming the joists (see page 51). If not, use a cordless drill to drive a screw through the subfloor and into the framing below. The easiest way to do this is with a special tool called a Squeeeeek No More. The tool guides the screw and controls how deep it's set.

Remove stains from carpet.

If you get to a stain early, getting it out should take only a few minutes. Start by blotting the area with a clean dry cloth, working from the outside edge of the stain toward the center. Put some lukewarm water on the stain and continue blotting until the stain, is gone or the cloth isn't absorbing any more of it. If necessary, mix 1/4 teaspoon of dishwashing liquid into 1 cup of lukewarm water, and pat it onto the area. After about five minutes, rinse the area with clear water and blot with a clean cloth. Put several white paper towels over the area and weigh them down.

Remove pet stains from carpet.

Even the best-trained pet can have an accident once in a while. This trick should keep your carpets in good shape and your pets out of the dog house: Blot up any liquid and pat the carpet with dishwashing liquid and water as described on page 57. Combine a tablespoon of white vinegar with a cup of water, and blot the mixture onto the area using a clean cloth. Weigh down white paper towels on the area, and leave them overnight.

Patch minor damage in carpet.

Small burns and stains don't have to spoil your carpet. To fix it, you need a carpet scrap and a handful of things from a home center or carpet retailer: an inexpensive "cookie-cutter" tool, double-stick carpet tape, and seam adhesive. Use the tool to cut a patch from the carpet scrap. Next, center the cutter over the stain, press down, and twist. Don't push too hard—you want to cut the carpet but not the pad. Cut a piece of double-stick carpet tape that spans the hole; remove the backing, and press the tape in place. Line up the nap or pattern, and set the patch in place. Apply seam adhesive to the edges of the patch and press it down.

Quick Tip Wearing clean socks or slippers indoors helps carpet stay clean. When you go barefoot, the natural oils in your skin and any lotion on your feet soak into the carpet and attract dirt and stains.

Reglue loose seams in carpet.

If a carpet seam works loose, buy some seam tape, and rent or borrow a seam iron from a carpet retailer. Pull up the old tape, then slide a strip of new tape under the seam, adhesive-side up. Heat up the seam iron. Pull back the edges of the carpet, and set the iron onto the tape, leaving it in place for about 30 seconds while the glue melts. Brush back the fibers on the two carpet flaps to keep them out of the glue, then press them together. (Work quickly—you have only about 30 seconds before the glue rehardens.) Work your way down the seam, repeating the process in segments that match the size of the seam iron. Place weights over the seam to keep it flat while the glue sets.

Quick Tip Direct sunlight fades carpet, hardwood, cork, and bamboo flooring. Rearrange the area rugs and furniture every six months or so to even out the floor's exposure to light.

Tile Floors

Protect your unglazed tile floors.

Most tile is covered with a glaze that protects it from stains and water damage. Some tile, such as terra cotta and tumbled stone, is left unglazed to create a more natural look. Unglazed tile needs to be sealed every year or two to protect it from stains and water spots. Large home centers and tile retailers carry a variety of sealers and can recommend the right type for your tile. Brush the sealer onto the tile, and let it dry according to the manufacturer's directions.

Clean grout joints in tile floors.

Grout, the material between the tiles, is vulnerable to mold, mildew, and stains. Use a soft-bristle brush and a mild, non-soap detergent to remove dirt and grime. Clear water and chlorine bleach (one part bleach to ten parts water) will remove mold and mildew.

Stone Floors

Remove stubborn stains from natural stone. When stains get tough, you've got to get tough with them. If your usual stone cleaner doesn't get the stain out, try a poultice (a special paste made to either draw the stain out or push it down into the stone). Spread the poultice on the stain, and then tape plastic wrap over it. Let the poultice set, according to manufacturer's instructions, then remove it. When the stain is gone, apply a stone sealer.

Vinyl Floors

Remove tough stains from vinyl or laminate flooring.
Stains like shoe polish, tar, or asphalt driveway sealer won't come out of vinyl or laminate flooring no matter how much you scrub with regular cleaners. You can get them out with a nail polish remover that contains acetone. Test the polish remover in a hidden area—under the refrigerator or stove, for example—before you tackle the stain. Using a clean cotton cloth, blot at the stain until it's gone, then wipe the area with a fresh cloth and plain water.

Fuse a small cut in sheet vinyl. Vinyl floors are extremely durable, but they can get damaged—if you drop a can of vegetables, for example. (And yes, this is the voice of experience speaking again.) A tube of liquid seam sealer, a clear compound available at home centers and flooring retailers, and a few minutes will solve the problem. V-shaped cuts are common, and the tip of the V sometimes curls back under itself. Pull the tip back into place with tweezers, then clean the area with lacquer thinner. Squeeze the seam sealer into the edges of the cut. When the sealer dries, the cut will be nearly invisible.

Patch large tears or burns in sheet vinyl. Fixing a large tear takes patience and the right tools, but it's not at all difficult. Tape a scrap of vinyl over the damaged area, with the patterns carefully aligned. Use a carpenter's square to draw a patch that follows the lines of the pattern (in the "grout lines" of a brick pattern, for example). Cut along the lines, using a utility knife to cut through both layers. Remove the scrap, and use a putty knife to pry up the damaged vinyl. Dissolve the old adhesive with mineral spirits, then scrape it off the subfloor with a putty knife. Spread new adhesive on the back of the patch, and press it into place. Roll the area with a J-roller, then let the patch dry a day. Fuse the edges of the patch with liquid seam sealer (see page 64).

> **Quick Tip** If you need to patch sheet vinyl and don't have a remnant, scavenge a piece from under an appliance or at the back of a closet. No one but you will ever know.

Replace a damaged vinyl floor tile.

A damaged vinyl tile is not a big problem, because you can replace the individual tile. The tools you need include a heat gun (something like a high-powered hair dryer), a putty knife, and a notched trowel. Soften the adhesive with the heat gun. Move the gun around quickly—the goal is to soften the adhesive, not melt the tile. When the adhesive is loose, use a putty knife to pry up the tile. Remove the remaining adhesive with mineral spirits and the putty knife. Spread new adhesive in the area with a notched trowel, then press a new tile in place. Wipe away any excess adhesive, and then roll the area with a J-roller.

Quick Tip It makes sense to buy tools you'll use a lot, but it may be better to rent tools that you won't need very often. A heat gun, for example, isn't necessary for a basic toolbox. Before investing in a tool like this, check with a local rental.

Stairs

Stop stairs from squeaking by nailing down the tread.
Beneath a set of stairs, notched boards called *stringers* provide support
for the *treads*, the boards you walk on. Like other parts of a floor,
stringers can shrink, swell, or get worn. When a stringer doesn't fit
snugly against the tread, the step can squeak. To fix this problem, add a couple of nails to secure the treads to the stringers. This can be done from above or beneath the stairs, depending on your best means of access. Drive the nails in at opposite angles, then countersink them.

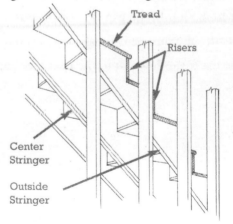

*Staircase construction: Hammer the tread to the
stringer to solve a squeaky stair problem.*

Stop squeaks by filling the gap between the tread and riser.

Sometimes a riser (the vertical board at the back of a step) shrinks, and the stair squeaks as the tread flexes up and down when you step on it. This one's easy to fix, as long as the underside of the staircase is exposed. Simply coat a hardwood shim with wood glue and use a hammer to tap it into the gap. Tap only until the shim is snug. If the ceiling beneath the staircase is finished, you can use a Squeeeeek No More to draw the tread down onto the riser (see page 56).

Stop squeaks by adding support between the tread and the riser.

If you have access to the underside of the stairs, this is an easy job. Use 2 x 4 wood scraps or cut some 6" blocks from a 2 x 4. Spread wood glue on top and along one edge of a block, and place it under the step where the tread meets the riser (the vertical board). Drive a couple screws to hold it to the squeaky tread, then drive a screw at an angle into the riser. Add blocks to both sides and the center of the step. The extra support should solve the problem.

Quick Tip To make stairs safer for children, install safety gates at the top and bottom of stairways. Use gates that screw to the wall instead of the ones that are held in by pressure. Before buying a gate, check for a certification seal from the Juvenile Products Manufacturers Association.

Tighten loose balusters.

The spindles of a railing are called *balusters*. Even though most square-top balusters are held in place by both wood glue and nails, they can work loose over time. Between each pair of balusters, directly below the rail, there is a small piece of wood trim, called a *fillet*, that helps hold the baluster in place. Chisel out the fillets on both sides of the loose baluster, then tighten a squeeze-type clamp onto the railing on one side, close to the baluster. At the top of the baluster, where it will be covered by the fillet, drill a pilot hole. Angle the hole so a screw can go through the baluster and up into the railing (see Figure A). Drive a one-inch wood screw through the pilot hole. Cut a new fillet, spread wood glue on top of the fillet, and clamp it in place. Tack the fillet in place with a couple of finish nails (see Figure B).

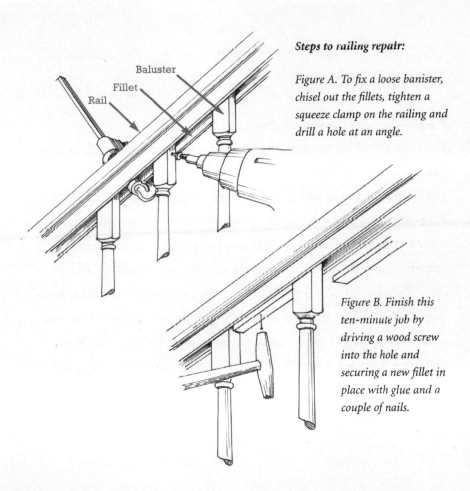

Steps to railing repair:

Figure A. To fix a loose banister, chisel out the fillets, tighten a squeeze clamp on the railing and drill a hole at an angle.

Baluster

Fillet

Rail

Figure B. Finish this ten-minute job by driving a wood screw into the hole and securing a new fillet in place with glue and a couple of nails.

Ceilings

Replace a damaged acoustical tile.

Most acoustical tile fits together with a tongue and groove. If the damaged tile isn't at an edge, you can't fit a new one into the surrounding groove edge, but you can get around that problem pretty easily if you have extra tiles or can buy a matching one. First, remove the damaged tile. (You may have to cut the tile into pieces to get it out.) Next, use a straightedge and a utility knife to cut off one of the tongues and the upper lip of the grooved edges of the new tile. Put a bead of construction adhesive on the furring strips at the edges of the hole where you removed the tile. Fit the remaining tongue into the adjacent groove, then press the tile up into the adhesive. Hold or prop the tile in place until the adhesive dries.

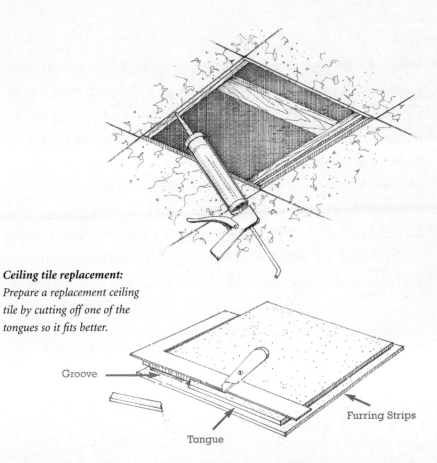

Ceiling tile replacement:
*Prepare a replacement ceiling
tile by cutting off one of the
tongues so it fits better.*

Groove

Tongue

Furring Strips

73

Patch a damaged drywall ceiling. Turn off the electrical circuit for the area. Draw a neat outline (a square or rectangle is best) around the damaged area, and use a drywall saw to cut it away. Cut a piece of plywood narrow enough to fit in the opening and long enough to reach about 2 inches beyond the edges. Use hot glue to attach the plywood to the back of the drywall, then reinforce each end with a couple of drywall screws. Cut a drywall patch to fit the opening, and use screws to attach it to the plywood backing. Cover the seams around the patch with self-stick drywall tape, and apply joint compound. When the joint compound is dry, sand the area, then prime and paint it. If it's a popcorn ceiling, use a spray can of ceiling texture to cover the patch. Restore the power.

Dust popcorn ceilings with lint rollers. You can't wash a popcorn ceiling, but you can clean it. You need two of those sticky lint rollers and a paint roller. Slide the lint roller sleeves over the paint roller, and roll lightly. Change the lint rollers when they stop picking up dirt.

Wash painted, textured ceilings. Use a cotton rag (a sponge will leave crumbs) and plain water to clean painted, textured ceilings.

Disguise stains on acoustical tile. Depending on the type of tile you have, it may be easier to camouflage small stains or marks than remove them. In an inconspicuous spot, test white shoe polish or correction fluid, such as Liquid Paper. If the color blends well, use it to cover the stain.

Chapter 3

Grand Openings

Windows and doors need to both look good and operate smoothly.
Neither issue is difficult, but both need your attention.

Windows
Cleaning Care

Make your windows sparkle.

Clean windows make the whole house look better, especially when they
sparkle! A professional window washer taught me this simple method
for making windows shine: Mix 1–2 tablespoons of original Dawn
dishwashing liquid into a gallon of warm water. Wipe the cleaning
solution onto the window with a lint-free rag. Starting at the top of the
window, use a squeegee to remove the cleaning solution. Dry the
squeegee after each stroke.

Quick Tip Direct sun dries the cleaning solution before you get it
wiped off, causing streaks. For streak-free windows, clean on a
cloudy day, or work in the opposite direction of the sun's movement
across your house.

Get your screens clean. Window screens are magnets for dust and dirt. Vacuum the screens, and then remove them. If possible, take the screens outside, and wash them with a hose and scrub brush. If not, wash them in a bathtub, and set them aside to dry. Vacuum and wash the woodwork with water and white vinegar before putting the screens back.

Quick Tip When you're washing both sides of a window, it can be hard to tell which side a streak is on, so you might end up redoing both. Forget about it: squeegee horizontally on one side and vertically on the other. If there's a streak, you can tell which side it's on by which way it runs.

Fix stubborn window cranks.

When you turn a window crank, it drives a system of rollers, extensions, and pivots. If these parts of the tracks are dirty, the window is

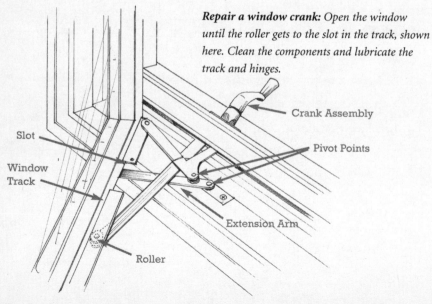

Repair a window crank: *Open the window until the roller gets to the slot in the track, shown here. Clean the components and lubricate the track and hinges.*

Crank Assembly

Slot

Pivot Points

Window
Track

Extension Arm

Roller

hard to operate. To clean a crank assembly, open the window until the roller at the end of the extension arm gets to the slot in the track. Pull the extension arm out of the track, and wipe off the roller. Clean the track with a stiff brush, and wipe off the pivoting arms and hinges. Spray a lubricant on the track and hinges, and wipe off any excess. Put the extension arm back into the track, and test the window. It should glide open and closed.

Adjust a double-hung window for easy opening and closing.

Modern double-hung windows (the kind where the sashes slide up and down to open and close) generally don't need much maintenance but do sometimes need to be adjusted. Start by cleaning the vinyl tracks with a toothbrush and a damp rag. While you're at it, look for the adjustment screw on the track insert on each side of the window. Turn these screws, a little at a time, until the window opens and closes smoothly.

Adjust the spring tension on double-hung windows.

To adjust a spring-lift window, unscrew the top end of the metal tube from the jamb, and twist it to adjust the spring tension. Holding the tube tightly, turn it clockwise for more lift, counterclockwise for less.

> **Quick Tip**
>
> Before you begin to sand or scrape the wood around your windows,
> be sure to buy a lead test kit. You can buy the test at any home store.
> If the test is positive, get expert advice before cleaning, sanding,
> scraping, or painting your windows or walls. You can find free
> brochures on dealing with lead paint in large paint departments; the
> government offers information at www.epa.gov.

STICKY SITUATIONS

Unstick a window by cutting the paint film.

I couldn't get the double-hung windows in my son's bedroom to open for the life of me. Finally, I realized that the previous owners had painted them shut. (Don't judge: It's an easy mistake to make.) Once I understood the problem, fixing it took only a few minutes. You can do it, too. Slip a paint zipper or utility knife between the window stop and the sash, and cut the paint film all the way down the window. (If you don't have a paint zipper, a pizza cutter will work almost as well.) Put a wood scrap against the side of each sash, and tap it lightly with a hammer. Ta da! The window should loosen. You may have to shove a bit, but it should now open. Clean up the cut paint with fine sandpaper, and sand the channels a little, too. Rub the channels with a bar of Ivory soap or paraffin wax—a white candle works great. Fresh air is now yours for the taking.

Unstick a window by cleaning the weatherstripping.

Another thing that makes double-hung windows stick is dirt or paint stuck to the weatherstripping. Spray some all-purpose cleaner on a clean rag, and wash the weatherstripping, working from the bottom to the top. To remove dried paint, use a clean rag and a little paint thinner. Be careful not to ruin the paint on the sashes and trim.

Unstick a window by finishing the wood.

If the window's not painted shut, and the weatherstripping is shiny clean, but the window still sticks, moisture may be making the wood swell. To protect the wood, all of the surfaces have to be painted or finished properly. If you find unfinished wood, that's the problem. Wait until the weather has been dry for a few days and the wood has shrunk a little, then paint or finish the wood.

CLIMATE CONTROL

Seal windows to keep in hot or cold air.

Gaps around windows let conditioned air get out and outside air get in, which costs you money. To seal the window casings (the wood trim around a window), apply clear silicone caulk to the joint between the casing and the wall.

Seal window sashes for extra savings.

During extremely cold or hot weather, sealing the gaps around window sashes also may reduce energy bills. Close and lock the window, then put clear, peelable caulk strips around the inside edges of the sashes. When the weather improves, remove the caulk.

Quick Tip Moisture between panels of sealed insulating glass is a sign
that the seal has failed. The window may need to be replaced.
Consult the window's manufacturer or a window retailer for advice.

Seal casement windows for added efficiency. Casement
windows are relatively energy-efficient, but you can improve their seals
by installing self-adhesive foam or rubber compression strips on the
outside edges of the window stops.

Eliminate condensation between removable glass panels.
Condensation forms between the panes of glass in windows with interior removable panels when the breather holes in the sash get plugged
with dust or dirt. Use a pipe cleaner or small wire to clean out the
holes in the bottom of the sash, and the condensation should disappear.

Prevent condensation on the room side of windows.
During cold weather, condensation forms on the room side of windows when the indoor air is too humid. If you're using a humidifier, turn it down or off. If that doesn't solve the problem, run a dehumidifier. (It's rare to need a dehumidifier in cold weather. If you do, make sure the clothes dryer is vented to the outside and that every member of the family is using the vent fan when they shower or bathe. If the problem continues, consult a heating and cooling contractor.)

Prevent condensation on the outside of windows.
When the temperature of the outer surface drops below the dew point of the outside air, moisture gathers on the outer glass of the window. This isn't really a problem, but the condensation obstructs your view and can leave spots and streaks. About the only thing you can do is to warm the glass by opening the drapes and blinds or turning up the thermostat.

DECOR

Hang curtains and drapes.

The exact instructions for hanging curtain rods and poles depend on their style, which is why they are sold with full instructions as well as the hardware, screws, and wall anchors you need. What the instructions may not tell you is where to put the rod or pole and how to work around unexpected developments. Before you go shopping, measure the window (be sure to include the surrounding trim in your measurement). Buy a rod or pole that's at least 12 inches longer than the window's width—this gives you 6 inches on each side for the curtains to hang when they're open. Now, before you try to install the rod, do a little investigation. Some windows are bordered above by reinforced concrete or steel beams, which makes drilling holes more than a little difficult. Drill a test hole about 6 inches above the top of the window. If everything goes well, you're ready to start following the product's instructions. If you run into major resistance, keep checking until you find the top of the reinforcement, and plan to install the hardware there. The other option is to attach the hardware to the window's frame, as long as the frame is wood.

Quick Tip A stud finder is inexpensive and invaluable. It lets you pinpoint the location of framing studs in moments. If you're decorating a home and will be hanging window treatments, pictures, and mirrors, add a stud finder to your toolbox.

Four Easy Ways to Childproof Your Windows

- Dangling window blind cords can be dangerous for children. Tie them up out of a child's reach or get a free fix-it kit at www.windowcoverings.org.

- Install window guards or safety stops on windows when there are children in the house. These items help to ensure that a child can not fall or climb out an open window. For windows on the sixth floor and below, choose guards that can be removed easily in case of emergency. On windows above the sixth floor, install window stops so the windows open no more than 4 inches.

- Always closely supervise children around windows.

- Never place a child's crib, playpen, or bed near a window.

Doors
KEEPING UP APPEARANCES

Refresh the entry with a clean front door.

Working from the top of the frame and down, vacuum the frame and the door. Wash the area with mild detergent and water. Use a sponge paintbrush to clean the corners of raised panels.

Cover scratches on stained wood doors.

Polish the door with an absorbent cotton rag and a specially formulated furniture polish, such as Old English Scratch Cover. The scratches will practically disappear, and the door will look new again.

Brighten door hardware with paste wax.

Wash grungy door hardware with mild detergent, then polish it with paste wax.

Fill cracks in wood doors.

Cracks are unattractive and expensive—they leak air! Luckily, they're easy to fix. On painted doors, fill the cracks with wood filler or caulk. On stained doors, use tinted wood putty. Work on the inside part of the door first. Sand each area as you finish and touch up the paint or stain.

Prevent cracks in wood doors.

Unless all the edges of a wood door are finished, it expands and contracts with the weather, which encourages cracks to form. To prevent this from happening, paint or seal all the edges of the door—including the top and bottom. You can find high-quality wood sealers in the parts department of a hardware store or home center or at any paint retailer.

Clean up the threshold.

When cleaning the front door, don't forget the threshold. One note: Never use any product containing ammonia on an aluminum threshold. You can wash almost any threshold with mild detergent (such as Tide) and water.

Refinish tarnished brass doorknobs and hardware.

Remove the tarnished pieces and soak them in a paint stripper that contains methylene chloride, following the manufacturer's directions. Lightly rub the hardware with #00 steel wool, then rinse it thoroughly. Clean it with brass cleaner, again following the manufacturer's instructions. Spray each piece with clear lacquer spray, and let it dry.

> **Quick Tip** Use fishing line to hang the hardware from a board or shelf so you can spray the finish on both sides.

Unstick stickers from wood doors and trim.

There are plenty of products that can remove stickers, but many of them also can remove wood's finish. Rather than risk that, soak the stickers with furniture polish, and let them sit for a few minutes. They should come right off. If not, repeat the process with cooking oil, mineral oil, or baby oil. If you don't have those things on hand, rubbing alcohol works, too.

Patch a small hole in a screen.

There's no end to the things that can create small holes in screens, children being the first that comes to my mind. Tiny holes don't seem to matter much until you realize these holes are magnets for mosquitoes and no-see-ums. Seal small holes in a fiberglass screen with clear nail polish. On a wire mesh screen, weave the edges of a mesh patch into the edges of the hole using a knitting needle or similar tool to push the wires in and out.

Adjust the closer on the storm door.

Automatic door closers keep storm doors from slamming closed. At least, they do if they're properly adjusted. To adjust the closer, find the adjustment screw, typically on the side that faces toward the door handle. Tighten or loosen the screw, and test the door until it closes completely but gently.

Add a wind chain to protect a storm door.

If a strong gust of wind catches an unprotected storm door, it can yank the hinges right out of the frame. To prevent this, install a wind chain that attaches to the door frame and the door to keep the door from opening more than 90°.

WEATHER WISE SOLUTIONS

Prevent drafts with a door sweep.

If the door sweep (a bristle or felt flap at the bottom of a door) is damaged or missing, cold air swoops in, and energy costs skyrocket. To replace or add a sweep, start by measuring the width of the door, so you can buy one that fits. Next, tack or tape the sweep in place on the inside of the door, positioned to touch the floor but not interfere with the door's operation. Drill pilot holes, and drive screws to hold the sweep in place.

Weatherstrip a sliding glass door.

Apply a self-adhesive rubber compression strip to seal the edge of the doorjamb of a sliding glass door.

Weatherstrip an exterior door.

Weatherstripping fills the gaps at the edges of a door to prevent drafts. Worn or missing weatherstripping costs you money every day. Self-adhesive products are easy to use, but it's really worth the effort to install metal weatherstripping. Measure the height and width of the door opening, and cut the metal strip to fit. Tack the strips to the doorjamb and to the header, inside the stops. Work from the top down. When the strips are in place, use a putty knife to pull them into position, between the door and the jambs, when the door is closed.

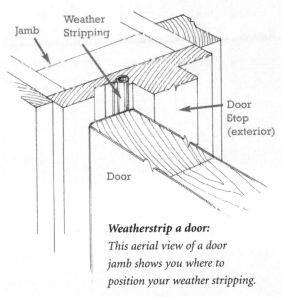

Weatherstrip a door:
This aerial view of a door jamb shows you where to position your weather stripping.

ADJUSTMENTS MADE EASY

Remove and rehang a door.

Recruit a helper to hold the door as you take out the hinge pins. Use a screwdriver and a hammer to drive the pins out of the hinges, starting with the bottom hinge and working up to the top one. If a hinge pin is stuck, drive it up and out from the bottom, using a nail set or a small screwdriver and a hammer. To rehang the door, reverse the process.

Tighten loose hinges.

If tightening the screws in the hinge doesn't fix the problem, it may mean the wood can no longer hold the screw tightly and needs to be filled. Small wood dowels and golf tees work perfectly for this. Remove the door. Coat the dowels/golf tees with wood glue, and tap them into the holes. When the glue is dry, use a utility knife to cut the dowel/tee flush with the surface. Drill pilot holes in the new wood, and rehang the door.

Adjust a bi-fold door.

Poorly adjusted bi-fold doors can drive you nuts—either they won't open, or they won't close. Either way, you can end up wanting to rip them off the track. Before you do something you'll regret, clean and adjust the door. With the doors open, clean the tracks, and then spray them, along with the rollers or pins, with a silicone lubricant. Close the doors, and check the gap between them. If it's not even, use a screwdriver or wrench to adjust the pivot blocks, which you'll find at the top or bottom of the doorframe. Tighten or loosen the pivot block, and recheck. Repeat until the gap between the doors is even.

Maintain sliding glass door tracks.

If a sliding glass door sticks, clean the tracks. Move the door to one side and then the other so you can vacuum the tracks and clean them with denatured alcohol. Spray the upper track with silicone spray and rub paraffin wax along the lower track.

Adjust a sliding glass door.

If the track is clean, and the door still sticks, clean and adjust the rollers. Slide the door to the middle of the tracks. Place a screwdriver into the access hole at the bottom of the door, and turn the adjustment screws to lower the rollers. Recruit someone to help you lift the door out of the track. Use a screwdriver to pry the rollers out of the door, then clean them with denatured alcohol, and spray them with silicone spray. When you're ready to replace the rollers, line up the adjustment screw with the access hole on the door. Put a block of wood in front of the rollers, and tap them into place with a rubber mallet. With your helper, guide the door into the top track, and then lift the bottom into the lower track. Slide the door to within half an inch of the latch-side jamb, and then turn the roller adjustment screws until the door is parallel with the jamb and the door latch lines up with the catch on the jamb.

Repair a stubborn sliding glass door:
*Turn the adjustment screws at the
bottom of the door as shown so you
can pry out the rollers and clean them.*

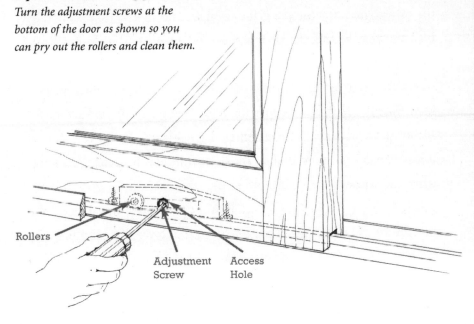

Rollers

Adjustment
Screw

Access
Hole

Square up a door.

When the gap on top of the door is radically wider on one side than the other, check the hinges. If they're tight and in good shape, the problem may be that the latch bolt on the door isn't lined up with the strike plate (the catch) on the frame. Open and close the door, and watch the relative placement of those two components. When you've identified the problem, remove the door (see page 98) and set it aside. If the strike plate needs to be higher, drive 3-inch wood screws into the top of the doorjamb to pull up the door frame; if it needs to be lower, drive the screws into the bottom of the jamb to pull the door frame down. To raise the latch bolt, install thin cardboard shims behind the bottom hinge, so it raises the whole door. To lower the door and the latch bolt, install shims under the top hinge.

Stop a door from sticking.

Don't struggle with a sticky door—fixing it only takes a few minutes. Before you do anything else, check the hinges, and make sure the door is square within the doorway (see page 98 and "Straighten a warped door" below). If these things check out, it's likely that the wood has swelled. Wait for a time when the weather has been dry for several days, and prepare for victory in this little battle. Close the door and mark where it hits the frame first. Remove the door (see page 98) and sand or plane the marked area. Rehang the door, and test it. When the door no longer sticks, seal the ends and edges with clear wood sealer.

Straighten a warped door.

Take the door down (see page 98), and lay it across a pair of sawhorses. Cover the bowed area with cushioning of some type—sturdy cardboard or a thick throw rug, for example—and place weights over it. Leave the weights in place until the door is straight. Put a coat of wood sealer on the edges of the door, and let it dry. Rehang the door.

Shorten an interior door. Shortening a door is something of a challenge, but it's absolutely possible if you take your time. A 3/8-inch gap is enough to let the door swing freely, so measure 3/8 of an inch up from the floor, and mark the bottom of the door so you know where to cut. Take the door down (see page 98), and set it across a pair of sawhorses. Extend the mark all the way across the bottom of the door, and then clamp a straightedge along the mark. Score along the straightedge with a utility knife, then cut along it with a circular saw. If the hollow core of the door is now exposed, chisel the veneer off the piece you just removed, and spread glue on it. Clamp it in place at the bottom of the door. When the glue is dry, rehang the door.

LOCKS AND PROTECTION

Burglar-proof your sliding glass door. Homeowners love sliding glass doors, because they let in lots of light. Burglars love them because they provide easy access. You can have the door without the danger if you attach it to the surrounding framing with sturdy pan-head screws. Drill pilot holes and drive a screw about every 8 inches along the top of the track; if the doorframe is metal, use self-tapping screws and a low drill speed. If thieves can't pry the door up and out of the lower track, they may move on to an easier target.

Quick Tip If you have deadbolt locks on your sliding glass doors, teach family members where the locks are and how to use them. In case of fire or other emergency, this information can save lives.

Attach a sliding-door lock.

Special deadbolt locks provide an extra measure of safety for sliding glass doors. Look for them at hardware stores and home centers. You'll need to follow the specific instructions on the lock you purchase, but the basic premise is that you attach the lock to the frame on the door's sliding panel and drill a hole for the deadbolt into the door's upper track. The extra security is worth the small amount of time and effort this takes.

Remove a doorknob.

It helps to understand how a doorknob works: The knob on one side has stems and a spindle that fit into holes in the knob on the other side. Screws from one knob fit into threads on the other to hold the pieces together. To remove a doorknob, hold both cover plates close to the door with one hand while you loosen the screws with the other. Pull the pieces apart, and set them aside.

Fix a sticky lockset.

A latch bolt—the part that extends from the doorknob into the door-frame—sticks when the screws that hold parts of the lockset together are too tight or the lockset needs lubrication. Loosen the connecting screws a little, and see if the latch works better. If not, remove the doorknob, and clean the inside. Spray an all-purpose lubricant into the mechanism, and reinstall the knob.

Install a doorknob.

After you fix a doorknob, the time comes when the pieces have to be put back together. Not a problem. Put the stem of the exterior knob into the hole in the latch case (the part that activates the latch bolt). Put the interior knob (the one with the lock, if it's a locking doorknob) on the spindle, and align the stems with the screw holes. Hold both covers against the door with one hand, and insert a screw into the screw hole closest to the door edge. Tighten this screw, then install the other one. Test the doorknob. If the latch bolt sticks, loosen the screws just a little.

Clean a deadbolt lock.

A deadbolt lock makes a home more secure, but if the deadbolt sticks or won't go all the way into the
strike plate, it doesn't protect anything. Most of the time, all a sticky deadbolt needs is a good cleaning. Loosen the screws on the cover plate of the inside latch and remove the inside and outside cylinders. Next, loosen the screws on the cover plate that surrounds the deadbolt, and remove the cover plate and deadbolt. Spray all-purpose lubricant on all the parts, then wipe away any excess lubricant. Reassemble, and check the lock.

Strengthen door hinges.

Another way to make it harder for burglars to kick in a door is to replace the short screws that typically hold the hinges to the door frame with 3- to 4-inch screws that will hold the hinge to the door-jamb and wall studs. When you drive the screws, be careful not to over-tighten them.

Quick Tip Keep kids out of unsafe or unsupervised areas by installing plastic door knob locks. The best ones keep kids from opening doors while still allowing adults to move freely about the home.

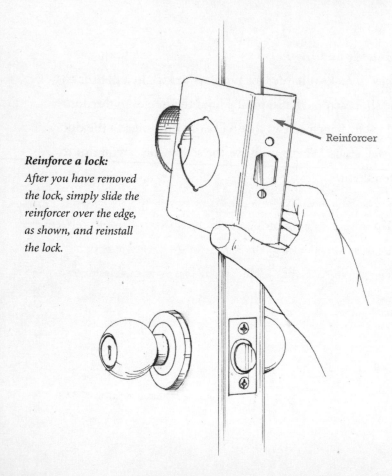

Reinforcer

Reinforce a lock:
After you have removed the lock, simply slide the reinforcer over the edge, as shown, and reinstall the lock.

Reinforce door locks. Many times, burglars don't bother trying to pick or jimmy locks—they simply kick in the door. Reinforcers make this more difficult, and smart burglars will move on to easier targets. Before you go to the hardware store or home center, measure the thickness of the door so you can buy a reinforcer that fits it. Remove the lock, and slide the reinforcer over the edge of the door. Reinstall the lock, and your home will be more secure.

Install a peephole. A peephole lets you see who's at the door before you open it, and installing one takes only a few minutes. You can find these devices at hardware stores and home centers, usually in the same aisle as the doorknobs and security locks. You need to follow the manufacturer's instructions for the model you buy, but the general idea is that you drill a hole completely through the door, then install one piece of the peephole from the outside and one from the inside. One piece simply screws into the other.

Chapter 4

Kitchens

The kitchen is the heart of a home—keeping it working right and looking good is essential.

Straighten crooked cabinet doors.

When the screws on the hinges work loose, cabinet doors end up hanging lower on one side than the other. Tightening the screws straightens the door.

Fix loose drawer pulls.

The holes behind drawer pulls wear out over time, too. Remove the drawer pull, and clean any dust or grime out of the worn hole. Mix up some powder-type putty (Durham's Rock Hard Water Putty is a good one), and use a putty knife to pack it into the hole. When the putty is completely dry, sand it flush with the surface, drill a pilot hole, and reattach the drawer pull.

Keep drawers from falling out.

Lots of people have kitchen drawers that clunk out of place if they're pulled out too far. Don't put up with this—most of the time you can fix the problem in a couple of minutes with nothing more than a screwdriver. Pull out the drawer and check the runners. The screws that hold the drawer runners to the cabinet carcass have probably worked themselves loose. Tighten all of them, and the problem should disappear. If the screw holes are damaged, try using larger screws. If that doesn't work, fill the holes with putty as described in the previous project.

Repair a drooping cabinet door.

Over time, hinge holes can get so worn that there's nothing left for the hinge screws to grip. If this happens, the cabinet door will start to droop. Don't worry—you won't believe how easy this is to fix. Take the door off (see page 98) and check out the holes—you need a wooden dowel or something else about the same size or slightly smaller. Wooden matches and golf tees often work great. Coat the dowels with polyurethane glue, such as Gorilla Glue, and tap them into the holes. (The glue will expand around the dowel to fill the hole.) Let the glue dry, then cut off the dowels flush with the surface. Drill a new pilot hole through the center of each dowel, and rehang the cabinet door.

Remove scratches from countertops.

Scratches and minor cuts can be removed from solid-surface countertops. Manufacturers supply sanding pads designed specifically for this job. Start with the medium grit-sanding pad; wet the area, and rub over the scratch in a straight line. After a few minutes, change the direction by 90°. Rinse off the sanding pad from time to time. Rinse off the countertop and repeat with the next finer grit pad, but cover a slightly larger area. Continue until the repair area blends into the surrounding countertop.

Clean a solid-surface sink.

Getting stains out of a solid-surface sink, the most common type of sink, is amazingly simple. Fill the sink with hot water and chlorine bleach, and let it soak for ten or fifteen minutes. Drain the sink, and then wash it with laundry detergent and dry it.

Clean a cast iron or china sink.

Wash the sink with soap or detergent. If necessary, use a soft abrasive cleaner, such as a paste made from baking soda and water.

Clean a stainless steel sink.
Start with soap or detergent and water. If that doesn't work, try a stainless steel polish and a soft cloth. Rub in the direction of the grain. Don't use bleach or cleaners that contain chloride on stainless steel.

Quick Tip Dish soap and bleach can be a dangerous combination. Be careful never to mix anything containing ammonia with chlorine bleach.

Unclog a kitchen sink with a garbage disposal.

Plunging a sink with a garbage disposal is exactly like plunging a sink without one, except for one thing: If there is an air gap, you need to block it off first. If you have an air gap, you'll find a chrome fitting, about 3 inches tall, next to the faucet. Look under the sink for the ribbed hose that connects the air gap to the garbage disposal. Put a quick clamp on the hose so water can't get through it, and you're ready to plunge the sink as usual (see page 119).

Clean a natural-stone sink.

Scrub the sink with a medium-bristle brush and a mild detergent and water. Don't use ammonia, strong detergents, abrasives, or vinegar on natural stone. If the sink is scratched, use a gentle abrasive powder to remove it. You can find the powder at hardware stores and home centers, usually in the cleaning aisle or displayed near the natural stone sink displays.

Unclog a kitchen sink without a garbage disposal.

Even I have to admit that this not much fun, but if you put on a good attitude along with your rubber gloves, it doesn't have to be tragic. Pull out anything you can reach in the drain, and—if it's a double sink—put the sink stopper in on the side that's not clogged. Rub some petroleum jelly on the rim of a plunger, and center its cup over the drain. If the water in the sink doesn't cover the cup, add water until it does. Push the plunger up and down with gusto, at least a dozen times.

Unclog a stubborn sink by cleaning the sink trap.

When a sink is clogged, the problem usually lies in the trap, the curved pipe under the sink. If plunging doesn't work, it's time to clean the trap. No one looks forward to this job, but it's not something to avoid like the plague. If you want to avoid germs and guck, however, pull on a pair of rubber gloves, and put a bucket under the trap before you start. Grip one of the slip nuts (the nuts that connect the pipe to the trap) with slip-joint pliers and turn counterclockwise until the nut is loose. Repeat with the slip nut at the other end of the trap. If your pipes are chrome or copper, slide the slip nuts down the pipe, and remove the washers. If the pipes are PVC, remove the slip nuts and the washers. Pull the trap loose and empty it into the bucket. You may have to use a stiff wire to pull out the clog. Wash the trap—in another sink, naturally—and reverse the process to replace it. Run some water to refill the trap.

> **Quick Tip** Use cold water when you run the garbage disposal. Warm water only partly dissolves grease, which lets a slimy residue build up inside the pipes. Cold water washes congealed grease down the drain and safely out into the sewer system.

Disinfect and deodorize your kitchen drain.

Once a month or so, mix a gallon of hot water with a cup of chlorine bleach and a tablespoon or two of laundry soap. Pour the solution down the drain, then run the hot water for a minute or so. If the sink is cast iron, china, or solid-surface materials, mix up the solution in the sink, and then open the drain. You'll clean both the sink and the drain in one step. If the sink is natural stone or stainless steel, mix the solution in a bucket, and carefully pour it down the drain.

Fix leaky sink pipes.

When a kitchen sink leaks, the seal between the strainer body and the drain opening is probably shot. Grab a pair of slip-joint pliers, a spud wrench, and some plumber's putty. First, unscrew the slip nuts on both ends of the tailpiece—the part that connects the strainer body to the sink trap—and remove it. Use the spud wrench to remove the locknut, and then remove the strainer assembly. (Take careful notes on the order of the parts as you take them apart. Generally, you'll find a plastic washer, locknut, friction ring, and rubber gasket between the

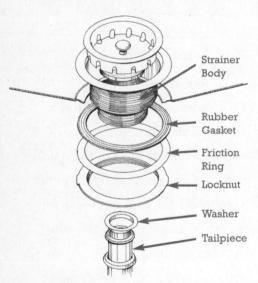

Strainer
Body

Rubber
Gasket

Friction
Ring

Locknut

Washer

Tailpiece

Get to know your sink: Sink leaks and other repairs are easier when you can identify the parts shown here.

tailpiece and strainer body.) Take the parts to a hardware store or home center and purchase replacements. Back at home, remove all the old putty from the lip of the drain opening, and apply a bead of new plumber's putty. Press the strainer body into the opening from above, then go under the sink to put the new rubber gasket and the friction ring over the strainer. Replace the locknut, and tighten it with the spud wrench; reinstall the tailpiece.

Quick Tip Pour several quarts of boiling water down the sink once a week. Water used for cooking works great. After you boil eggs, cook pasta, or make tea, pour leftover water down each kitchen sink drain.

Energize a sink sprayer.

Unscrew the aerator from the sprayer, and clean it with a toothbrush and vinegar. If the holes are filled with mineral deposits, soak the aerator in the vinegar overnight, then reassemble the sprayer.

Repair the valve on a weak sink sprayer.

The diverter valve, located inside the faucet body, directs water from the faucet to the sprayer. If a clean sprayer isn't putting out enough water, the diverter valve may be worn out. Turn off the water at the shutoff valves, then loosen the setscrew, and remove the faucet handle and spout. Use needle nose pliers to pull out the diverter valve, the small round piece at the front of the faucet body. Clean the valve with a toothbrush and vinegar. Coat new O-rings and washers with heat-proof grease, and then reassemble the diverter valve and faucet body. Turn the water back on.

Replace a sprayer hose.

The time may come when it's easier to replace your sprayer than to fix it. First, turn off the water at the shutoff valves under the sink. While you're under the sink, use slip-joint pliers to unscrew the hose from the faucet body. Working from above, pull the hose up through the opening where it sits. When you have the hose free, unscrew the sprayer head, and take the washer off of the end of the handle-mount. When the washer is off, you'll see a small metal retaining clip that holds the handle mount onto the end of the hose. Use needle nose pliers to remove that clip, and then slide the mounting off the end of the hose. Attach the handle mount, retaining clip, washer, and sprayer head to one end of the new hose, and then attach the other end to the faucet.

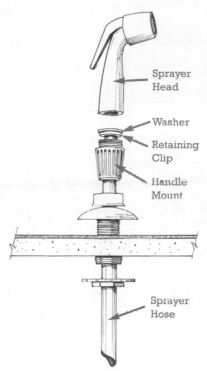

Sprayer Head

Washer

Retaining Clip

Handle Mount

Sprayer Hose

Sprayer hose assembly: *To replace a sprayer hose once it's been detached from the faucet body, simply remove these parts and attach them to the new hose.*

Repair a pullout spout.

A pullout spout is a sink faucet that switches to a sprayer as needed. Turn off the water at the shutoff valves (see page 178), and tie the sprayer hose, to the handle so it can't fall through the faucet body. Unscrew the spout head from the hose and check the rubber washers. If they're worn or damaged, replace them. Scrub the in-line screen with a toothbrush and vinegar. If the screen is filled with mineral deposits, soak it in vinegar; if it's damaged, replace it. Check and clean the aerator in the same way, if necessary. Reassemble the pieces, and you're back in business.

> **Quick Tip** To freshen your garbage disposal, mix a gallon of hot water with a tablespoon or two of laundry detergent and pour it down the drain while the disposal is running. Next, grind up several hands full of ice cubes. Finish by grinding up half a lemon or lime. The disposal should now be clean and smell fresh.

Fix a non-responsive disposal.

If the disposal doesn't respond at all when you turn it on, look under the unit for the reset button, typically a small, red, square button. If you push the reset button and the disposal still doesn't work, check the circuit breaker or fuse. If that doesn't help, it's time to call the repair person.

Free a jammed disposal.

A jammed disposal won't run, but the motor hums when you turn it on. To unjam it, you need to get the impeller assembly to turn. Before you do anything else, turn off the electricity to the unit. If the disposal is hard-wired, turn off the circuit. If it's plugged into a receptacle under the sink, simply unplug it. Insert an Allen wrench into the slot at the bottom of the disposal, and turn it clockwise for several revolutions. Restore the electricity, and test the disposal. If all else fails, make sure the electricity is off, and put a broomstick down into the unit, and try to turn the blades using the end of the broomstick. Restore the electricity, and test the unit. If it still doesn't work, call a repair person.

Clean refrigerator coils.

Cleaning the coils every season saves energy and helps the refrigerator last longer. Roll the refrigerator away from the wall, and unplug it. Use a brush attachment on a vacuum cleaner to clean dust and lint from the coils on the back of the unit. Next, remove the plastic panel on the front of the refrigerator, at the bottom. Typically, this panel snaps off, but you may need to remove a couple screws to get it off. Use a crevice attachment to clean the coils behind the panel. Clean the floor, plug the refrigerator in, and roll it back into position.

Maintain a refrigerator gasket.

You can extend the life of a refrigerator gasket by giving it a little tender loving care a couple of times a year. Clean the gasket with soapy water and a damp rag. Dry it, and then put a little petroleum jelly on your finger, and spread it around the gasket to keep it lubricated and prevent cracking.

Check the seal on a refrigerator door.

Rubber gaskets around refrigerator and freezer doors seal the cold air inside. If the gasket is worn out, the compressor has to work overtime to keep up, which is expensive and hard on the unit. A couple of times a year, check the seal for cracks or other damage. Hold a dollar bill at the door's edge, and close the door. Pull the dollar out: You should feel the gasket grip the dollar. If it slips out without resistance, the gasket may need to be replaced. Consult a repair person for the actual replacement.

Replace a light bulb in a refrigerator.

Since the light is on only when the door is open, the bulb can last for many years, but when it finally burns out, you can replace it easily. Look inside the refrigerator, and find the bulb housing, often at the top, near the front of the unit. Snap off the bulb cover, and unplug the refrigerator before unscrewing the bulb. Take it to a hardware store or home center to find an exact replacement. Install the new bulb, and replace the cover.

Level a refrigerator.

In order for refrigerator doors to close properly the unit needs to be level. To check, set a level across the top of the unit, near the front and running from right to left. If the bubble on the level is in the center of the black lines, the refrigerator is level. If not, you need to adjust the front feet. Pull off the lower panel on the front of the refrigerator, and find the feet. If the bubble is off to the right, you'll want to raise the right foot or lower the left. If it slopes to the left, you'll need to do the opposite. To adjust the feet, use an adjustable wrench to turn the screw. Turn the screw clockwise to lower a foot, counterclockwise to raise it. Adjust the feet until the bubble is directly in the center.

Keep your gas burners firing.

Keeping the burners clean and the gas orifices open helps gas burners work efficiently. If burned-on food is stuck in the holes, remove the burner, and use a thin wire to clean out the holes.

Clean the grease filter on a hood-mounted microwave.

Most hood-mounted microwaves have two-part grease filters: a metal filter on the bottom of the unit and a charcoal screen beneath that. Every month or two, take out the metal filter, and run it through the wash cycle only in the dishwasher. Let the filter air dry completely before replacing it. The charcoal filter can't be cleaned, so it needs to be replaced every six months or so. You can find replacement filters at appliance and hardware stores.

Replace an electric burner element.

A burner element (the part of an electric stove that heats up) is easy to replace—most simply plug into the stove. To remove this type of burner, lift the front edge, remove the chrome ring, and pull the burner free. Take the burner along to an appliance store or home center, and buy an exact replacement. Plug the new burner into the stove, and all's well. Burners that are attached with screws should be replaced by a service person.

Fix the light bulb in an oven.

Contrary to what my children deeply believe, there is no little guy inside the oven, turning the light on and off. Instead, there is a little switch near the top of the door. When the door is closed, the switch is depressed, and the light goes off. When the door is opened, the switch pops up, and the light turns on. Sometimes food splatters on the switch and gets baked in place, which jams the switch closed. Clean the area, and see if that fixes the problem. If not, remove the light bulb, and take it to the hardware store or home center to find an exact replacement. Replace the bulb, and try again. If this doesn't solve the problem, it's time to call a repair person.

Fix a leaky dishwasher door.

If the catch doesn't close completely, the door will leak. Loosen the screws holding the catch in place, reposition the catch, and retighten the screws.

Clean a self-cleaning oven.

Self-cleaning ovens are marvelous. Turn a couple of dials, and the oven does most of the work. The only thing you have to do first is remove the racks, scrape off any burned-on deposits, and follow the manufacturer's instructions to lock the door and start the cycle. When the cycle is over, and the oven has cooled, wipe down the walls and floors of the oven with a damp rag or sponge. To clean the oven racks, put them in a big garbage bag along with a cotton rag soaked in ammonia. Tie a knot in the top of the bag, and put the bag outside or in the garage for the night. Wash the racks in hot water, and return them to the oven.

Sanitize a dishwasher.

Clean out the dishwasher once a year or so. Turn off the power to the dishwasher, and take out the racks so you can get to the strainer at the bottom of the unit. Remove any screws holding it in place, and pull out the strainer. Use a dishwashing liquid and an old toothbrush to scrub it clean. Next, unscrew the sprayer tower and the spray arm. Use a paper clip or small wire to unclog the holes on both sides of the spray arm. Soak the arm in vinegar first if the deposits are unusually stubborn. Rinse off the tower and spray arm, and reassemble the parts. Restore power, add dishwashing detergent, and run the empty dishwasher through a wash cycle.

Replace a door gasket on a dishwasher.

Dishwashers also leak when the door gasket wears out. Check the gasket for cracks, tears, or other damage. If it needs to be replaced, shut off power to the dishwasher, pull out the racks, and remove the retaining hardware (usually screws or clips). Take the gasket to a hardware store or home center and buy an exact replacement. Soak the new gasket in warm soapy water. When it feels pliable, position one end at the center of the door, and press or slide the gasket into the track. Refasten the retaining hardware as you go.

Replace a dishwasher hose.

Like any other hose, the hoses connecting the dishwasher to the water supply and drain can get brittle or damaged over time. Every couple of years, replace these hoses. Typically, they're secured with spring-type clamps. Remove the clamps, and pull off the hoses. Take the hoses to the hardware store or home center, and buy exact replacements. Slip the clamps onto the hoses, work the ends onto the respective nipples, and tighten the clamps in place.

Chapter 5

Bathrooms

Most of us start and end our days in the bathroom. This room should always be pleasant, comfortable, and in good repair.

Fill a chip in a porcelain or enamel sink.

Porcelain and enamel sinks are pretty durable, but accidents happen. There's no reason to ignore a chipped sink—you can buy a porcelain or enamel repair kit at any hardware store or home center. Most of these kits include filler and paint that you brush on like nail polish.

Fill a crack in a porcelain or enamel sink.

Buy some epoxy adhesive at a hardware store or home center. (Be sure to get the kind designed for sink repairs.) Dry the surface of the sink with a hair dryer. Mix the two parts of the epoxy, following manufacturer's instructions. Use a toothpick or stiff wire to spread the epoxy in the crack. Smooth out the epoxy as much as possible. Let the epoxy cure. Drying times vary a little from one manufacturer to another, but usually this takes about 24 hours. Be sure to read and follow package instructions. When the epoxy is ready, touch up the cracked area with appliance paint that matches the sink's color.

Fix the sink stopper on sinks with a lift rod. If your stopper isn't tight enough, and your sink won't hold water, you may need to adjust the lift rod, the rod you pull up and push down to open and close the stopper. It's attached to the back of the clevis strap and held in place with a screw. Turn the screw counterclockwise, and adjust the lift rod until the stopper is closed when the lever is all the way up. Tighten the screw and test the stopper. (If the screw is stuck, spray it with lubricating spray and let it sit for a few minutes.) Repeat if necessary.

Fix a pop-up drain stopper. A pop-up sink stopper is linked to an ingenious mechanism that raises and lowers the stopper to open and close the drain. If the sink doesn't hold water or the stopper doesn't pop up, the pivot rod needs to be adjusted. Look under the sink: you'll see a small metal rod (the pivot rod), that extends from the drain pipe into a hole in a narrow metal strip (clevis strap) and is held in place with a V-shaped clip (spring clip). To adjust the pivot rod, pinch the spring clip, and pull it off. Move the pivot rod into a different hole, replace the spring clip, and test the drain.

Fix a pop-up drain stopper:
Moving the pivot rod into a different hole in the clevis strap should get your pop-up stopper working again.

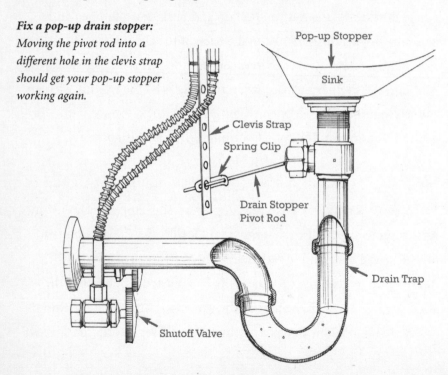

Pop-up Stopper

Sink

Clevis Strap

Spring Clip

Drain Stopper Pivot Rod

Drain Trap

Shutoff Valve

Replace a pop-up drain stopper.

If adjusting the pivot rod and lift rod doesn't solve the problem, it may be time to replace the whole thing. (I once went ten rounds with a stopper only to find that the pivot rod was completely corroded and couldn't be fixed.) This sounds complicated, but I promise it's not. Take a deep breath and get going. Loosen the nut holding the pivot rod into the drain pipe and the screw holding the lift rod into the clevis strap, and

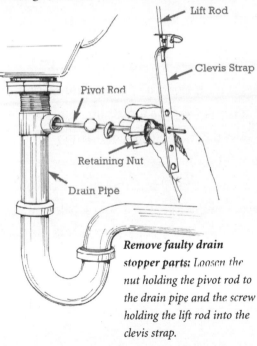

Remove faulty drain stopper parts: Loosen the nut holding the pivot rod to the drain pipe and the screw holding the lift rod into the clevis strap.

remove the mechanism. Take it to a hardware store or home center, and buy a replacement. Thread the lift rod into the clevis strap, and tighten the screw; insert the ball-end of the pivot rod into the drain pipe and tighten the nut. Set and adjust the pivot rod in the clevis strap.

Retrieve a treasure that's fallen down a drain.

Most of us close the drain before we put on or take off jewelry near a sink, but everyone forgets now and then. If an earring or ring slips down the drain, spring into action. Above all, *don't run the water*. Each time you run water, some of it stays in the trap, the curved section of pipe below the drain. If you're lucky, your treasure is sitting in the water in the trap. Put a bucket below the trap and remove it (see page 145). Turn the trap upside down in the bucket and check for your treasure. If it's not in the trap, your only hope is that it's stuck in the drain. Cross your fingers, and run a little water down the drain. Good luck.

Unclog a sink with non-toxic chemicals.

Chemical drain cleaners are effective but hazardous. Before you use one, try this simple formula instead: Pour a cup of baking soda into the drain, then add a pint of vinegar. Stand back—foam will erupt from the drain. After about fifteen minutes, pour several cups of boiling water down the drain. This will do the trick on many clogs.

Unclog a sink when chemical drain cleaners fail.

If you use chemical drain cleaners, and they don't unclog the drain, they will leave caustic chemicals behind in the sink trap. At that point, you are stuck: Plunging the sink might cause chemicals to erupt from the drain, and removing the trap also could be tricky, since those same chemicals will be mixed into the water inside the trap. The smartest thing to do when chemical drain cleaners fail is to call a plumber and warn them about the situation before they start working. If you insist on plunging the sink, wear protective clothing, including gloves and eye protection.

Plunge a bathroom sink.

Most clogs in bathroom sinks are made up of hair and soap scum, so plunging the sink usually creates enough pressure to push the clog down the drain. First, take out the stopper, and stuff a wet rag into the overflow opening located on the inside of the sink bowl opposite the faucet. Plunging is more effective when you block air from reaching the drain through this opening. Next, put a little petroleum jelly around the lip of the plunger, and place the cup over the drain opening. If the water in the sink doesn't cover the cup, add more. Push the plunger up and down, using enough force to make progress but not enough to damage the sink or drain. When the clog is clear, run the hot water for a minute.

Quick Tip To remove a pop-up stopper, try lifting it out. If that doesn't work, turn the stopper clockwise before pulling it out. If it still doesn't come out, get under the sink, and loosen the pivot rod before you try again.

Promote healthy drains.

Mix up a batch of this formula, and use it in each drain in the house—including tub drains—once a week. Combine a cup of baking soda, a cup of salt, and 1/4 cup of cream of tartar. To treat a drain, wash a quarter cup of the mixture down the drain with two cups of boiling water.

Clean out the sink trap.

Just like the clogs in kitchen sinks, some clogs in bathroom sinks are too stubborn to be pushed out by non-toxic chemicals or a plunger. The only solution is to remove the trap and clean it out. Pull on a pair of rubber gloves, and put a bucket under the trap. Grip one of the slip nuts with slip-joint pliers, and turn counterclockwise until the nut is loose; loosen the slip nut at the other end of the trap. If your pipes are chrome or copper, slide the slip nuts down the pipe, and remove the washers. If the pipes are PVC, remove the slip nuts and the washers. Pull the trap loose, and use a stiff wire to pull or push out the clog. Wash the trap, and reverse the process to replace it. Run some water to refill the trap.

> **Quick Tip** Chrome and copper sink traps can corrode over time. After removing an old trap, take it to a hardware store and home center and buy a replacement. Traps don't cost much, and it's better to replace a doubtful one than to clean up the mess if it falls apart later.

Remove old caulk from sinks and tubs.

Holes or cracks in the caulk around a sink or tub give water a path under counters, into walls, or under floors. The results—water damage, mold, mildew—are not pretty. Before you remove failed caulk, put painter's tape above and below the caulk to keep from scratching up the sink, the tub, or the surrounding tile. Use a utility knife or flathead screwdriver to scrape away the caulk. Use bleach to remove any mold or mildew underneath. Dry the area completely with a clean rag.

Caulk a sink.

Caulk creates a seal between a drop-in sink and the surrounding countertop and keeps water from damaging the countertop. If the caulk in this joint starts to deteriorate, replace it as soon as possible. Start by removing the old caulk (see page 146). With the painter's tape still in place, squeeze a thin bead of caulk along the joint. Use your index finger to smooth out the caulk, then remove the tape. Wipe away any excess caulk with a damp rag.

Caulk a bathtub.

Remove the old caulk if there is any (see page 146). Tape above and below the joint that needs caulking, and fill the tub with water. This weighs the tub down and opens up the joint so you can fill it deeper. Squeeze a thin bead of caulk along the open joint. Use your index finger to smooth out the caulk. Remove the tape, and wipe away any excess caulk with a damp rag.

Replace a tub spout.

In a combination tub and shower, the tub spout has a mechanism that diverts the water from the tub spout to the showerhead. When a diverter stops working, replace the tub spout. Look under the spout. If you see an access slot, the spout is held in place by a setscrew; use an Allen wrench to remove the screw and slide the spout off the nipple. If you don't see an access slot, the spout is screwed directly onto the nipple. Put a large screwdriver or hammer handle into the spout, and turn the whole thing counterclockwise. The stem sticking out of the wall is known as a *spout nipple.* Spread pipe joint compound or wrap Teflon tape on the threads of the nipple, and reverse the process to install the new spout.

Unclog a pop-up tub drain.

A pop-up tub drain has a metal drain stopper that moves up and down to open and close the drain. To clean a pop-up tub drain, open the stopper, and carefully pull the assembly from the drain opening. Clean it with a small wire brush. Next, take out the screws on the sides of the coverplate, and remove the cover plate and attached hardware. Clean the assembly with a small wire brush, lubricate it with heatproof grease, and reinstall it.

Adjust a pop-up tub drain so the tub holds water.

Remove the stopper and overflow assemblies (see page 139). Check out the linkage assembly attached to the back of the cover plate. You'll see a threaded rod, known as a *lift rod*. Loosen the locknut on the lift rod, and screw the rod up about 1/8 of an inch. This should help close the gap between the stopper and the drain. Tighten the locknut. Reinstall the tub drain assembly, and test it.

Unclog a plunger-type tub drain.

A plunger-type drain is covered by a fixed drain cover. Inside the drain, a brass plug opens and closes the drain. Remove the screws, and carefully pull off the cover plate and attached hardware. Clean the assembly with a small wire brush, and lubricate it with heatproof grease. Reinstall the assembly, and tighten the screws on the cover plate.

Maintain a whirlpool tub.

Cleaning a whirlpool tub and flushing the system regularly kills the mold and bacteria trying to take up residence in the plumbing. Use a nonabrasive cleaner and plain water to remove soap residue, oils, and mineral deposits from the tub's surface. To flush the system, fill the tub with hot water and add a little dishwasher detergent. Run the pump for ten or fifteen minutes, then drain the tub and refill it with cold water. Run the pump for ten more minutes. (Check the manufacturer's recommendations for suggested cleaning product.)

Adjust a plunger-type tub drain so the tub holds water.

Remove the drain assemblies (see page 150), and check out the linkage assembly. Use a pair of needle nose pliers to loosen the locknut on the threaded lift rod. Screw the rod down about 1/8 of an inch, and retighten the locknut. Reinstall the drain assembly.

Fix a severely clogged showerhead.

Sometimes mineral deposits get so far out of hand that a showerhead's water pressure is radically reduced, or it sprays off in funny directions. If this happens, it's time to go to Plan B. Remove the showerhead and the collar nut using an adjustable wrench or slip-joint pliers. Clean out the inlet holes with the end of a paper clip, then rinse them with clean water. Soak the whole piece in white vinegar for an hour or so to remove any deposits inside. Reassemble the showerhead, and test it. The spray should be much better.

Quick Tip Every household needs two plungers: one for sinks, tubs, and showers and another for toilets. Color code or label the handles so they don't get mixed up.

Fix a clogged showerhead the easy way.

Over time, mineral deposits form on the holes of a showerhead—especially if you have hard water. If you don't let them build up too much, you can clean out the deposits with little effort. Before you go to bed, fill a plastic sandwich bag with white vinegar, and fasten it around the showerhead. (A rubber band will hold it in place.) In the morning, the deposits should be things of the past.

Plunge a shower drain.

If you can't remove the clog with a wire, use a plunger to blast it out. Put a little petroleum jelly on the lip of the cup, and place it over the drain opening. Run the shower until there's enough water in the shower floor to cover the lip of the cup. Push the handle up and down a dozen times or so. Put some energy into it! Run some more water into the shower, and watch to see what happens. If the drain's still running slowly, plunge again until you're satisfied with the results.

Remove a hair clog from a shower drain.

Dermatologists say that the average person loses more than 100 hairs per day. No wonder most clogs in shower drains are caused by hair—a family of four washes several hundred hairs down there every day. When a shower drain starts running slowly, pry up the drain cover with a screwdriver, and use a piece of stiff wire to fish out the hair you can reach. (I untwist a coat hanger and shape the hooked end to fit into the drain.)

153

Quick Tip Before using pliers or a wrench on metal pipes or faucets, cover their jaws with masking tape so they don't scratch the finish.

Fix a drooping showerhead.

Inside a pivoting showerhead, there is an O-ring that seals the pivot head against the swivel ball. If that O-ring wears out, the showerhead won't stay where you put it. This is a small aggravation, but there's no reason to tolerate it. Remove the showerhead (see page 151), and pull off the O-ring (the rubber ring inside the pivot head). Take the O-ring to a hardware store or home center, and get a replacement. Lubricate it with heatproof grease before you slip it into place. Reinstall the showerhead, and congratulate yourself when it stays put next time you shower.

Seal tile grout.

Tile—whether ceramic, porcelain, or stone—repels water naturally, but grout (the filler between the tiles) does not. Grout sealer, which is available at tile retailers, hardware stores, and home centers, helps grout shed water so it resists mold and mildew. If you're not sure whether or not the grout in a shower has been sealed, put a few drops of water on a grout line. If the water beads up, the grout is sealed. If the water soaks right in, you've got a little work to do. Buy a bottle of sealer and a couple small sponge brushes. Brush the sealer onto the grout lines only, not the tile. After a year or so, test the grout from time to time, and reseal as needed.

Quick Tip If you see gaps or cracks in the grout or caulk of your shower, remove and replace it as soon as possible. Removing grout isn't difficult, but it takes much longer than ten minutes! Not as much time, however, as fixing the damage caused by water leaking through the holes and cracks.

Remove mold and mildew from the shower.

Mix 1 cup of chlorine bleach and ½ a cup of laundry detergent into 1 gallon of hot water. Brush the mixture onto the moldy areas, and let it sit for 10 minutes. Scour the area with a soft-bristle brush and clear water.

Replace a shower or bathroom wall accessory.

Start by scraping away the grout from the surrounding joints, using a utility knife or the pointed end of a can opener. Working carefully, pry out the accessory with a hammer and chisel. Scrape down the opening with a putty knife or a utility knife. Spread dry-set tile adhesive on the back of the new accessory, and press it firmly into place. Wet adhesive won't hold the accessory in place, so you need to support it with several strips of masking tape. Run long strips of tape from the wall, across the accessory, and down to the wall again. When the adhesive has cured (check label directions for curing times), grout the area.

Keep a shower clean.

The best way to keep a shower fresh is to wipe down the walls with a squeegee after you shower. Keeping the shower walls dry will keep mold and mildew from forming. If more than one person uses the shower in the morning, only the last person really needs to dry the shower (Yet another reason to get up early!).

Tighten up towel bars.

Behind most surface-mounted towel bars, there is a mounting clip screwed to the wall. The towel bar is held to the clip by a setscrew on the base at each end of the bar. When a towel bar wiggles or wobbles, those little screws need to be tightened. If you don't see the screws right away, kneel down and check from below the bar—often they're located down where they can't be seen.

Remove stains from ceramic tile.

Rinse the stained area with clear water. Add a little bleach to a cup of baking soda, and stir it to make a paste. Open a window or turn on the bathroom fan, and pull on rubber gloves. Scrub the stains with the paste, and then rinse the area with clear water.

Unclog a toilet.

Place the cup of the plunger over the toilet's drain opening, and push it up and down 15 to 20 times. Plunge energetically but not too forcefully. You don't want to crack the basin. If there isn't much water in the bowl, add a quart or so of water to help flush the clog through the drain. If plunging doesn't push the clog through the pipe, you may be able to create a vacuum that will suck the clog into the bowl, where you can remove it. Push the plunger down over the drain opening, and then pull it up quickly to create a vacuum.

Quick Tip Every sink and toilet in your house should have shut-off valves. Shut-off valves give you a way to turn off the water if a clogged toilet is overflowing or a faucet needs repairs. If you don't see handles at the end of the water supply lines beneath a toilet or sink, consult a plumber right away.

Fix a toilet handle that sticks.

Take the lid off the toilet, and locate the handle mounting nut. Grip the nut with an adjustable wrench, and turn it clockwise. When you get it off, scrub it inside and out with a toothbrush and warm vinegar.

Stop a running toilet by adjusting the lift chain.

A friend of mine posted this misspelled note on her toilet: "This toilet runs. Giggle the handle." Trust me on this: It's easier to fix a toilet that won't stop running than make its handle giggle. Take the lid off the toilet tank, and look inside. You'll find that the handle is attached to a handle lever, which in turn is attached to a lift chain or, on some toilets, lift wires. If the toilet has a lift chain, adjust it until it hangs straight down from the handle, with about a ½ an inch of slack in the chain. If the toilet has lift wires, they may be bent. Straighten them, and the toilet should work correctly.

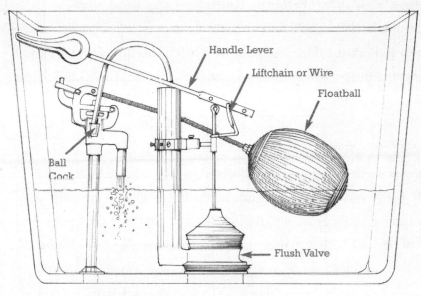

Handle Lever

Liftchain or Wire

Floatball

Ball Cock

Flush Valve

Toilet tank interior: *Minor adjustments to the lift chain, lift rod, float arm, or flush valve can fix a running toilet.*

Stop a running toilet by adjusting the float arm.

Inside the toilet, you'll find a *float ball*, a copper or rubber ball attached to a rod called a *float arm*. If the float ball is too close to the tank wall, it could make the water run nonstop. Bend the float arm until the ball is no longer touching the tank wall.

Stop a running toilet by adjusting the flush valve.

If you've adjusted the lift chain and the float ball, and the toilet is still running, you may want to try cleaning and adjusting the flush valve. Lift the tank ball or flapper (the rubber seal hanging from the handle lever), and clean the opening of the flush valve. Finally, loosen the screw that holds the guide arm, and adjust the tank ball (or flapper) until it's directly over the flush valve.

Tighten up a leaky toilet tank.

When a toilet tank leaks, the simplest possibility is that one of the connections is loose. Start with the tank bolts, which connect the tank to the base in a two-piece toilet. (If this is a one-piece toilet, skip this part.) You need an adjustable wrench to tighten the bolts and a light touch—if you tighten the bolts too much, you could crack the tank. Go slow and easy, and you'll be fine. Next, look for the water supply line at the bottom of one side of the tank. Tighten the nuts at the top and bottom of the connection between the line and the tank.

Check the wax ring in a leaky tank.

If you notice water around the base of the toilet, especially if the water shows up right after the toilet is flushed, the wax ring may be worn out. This one's easy to diagnose but not so easy to fix. Pour a couple of drops of food coloring in the tank, and flush the toilet. If colored water leaks onto the floor, you can be pretty sure the wax ring is broken. It's time to call a plumber.

Stop condensation from forming on a toilet tank.

If a tank leaks only during humid weather, condensation may be forming on the tank. Go to a hardware store or home center, and get a tank liner kit. Turn off the water at the shut-off valves behind the toilet, flush the toilet until the tank is empty, and clean the inside walls with a scrubbie pad and a mild abrasive cleaner. Cut the insulation panels to fit the front, back, sides, and bottom of the inside of your toilet tank. Attach the panels to the walls of the tank with the adhesive provided in the kit. Turn the water back on at the shut-off valves, and refill the tank.

Improve a toilet's flushing power.

Part of a toilet's flushing power comes from water flowing through dozens of little holes under the rim. If they're clogged with mineral deposits or just plain dirt, the toilet doesn't flush as well as it should. Grab your rubber gloves and a thin wire. Poke the wire into each hole, force out the dirt or deposits, and then scrub under the rim with a small, elongated brush. The flush should now be much stronger.

Replace a toilet seat.

Look under the rim of the toilet base to find the nuts that hold the bolts that hold the toilet seat that lives in the house that Jack built. No, no, that's another story, but you *will* find the nuts under the rim of the base, near the back. If the nuts are hard to turn, spray them with lubricating oil, wait a few minutes, then remove them with a ratchet wrench or an adjustable wrench. Pull out the old bolts, and take off the old toilet seat. Put the new seat in place, and insert the bolts through the hinges and the holes in the base. Slide new washers up the bolts, and carefully tighten the nuts. Go slow and easy—the base can crack if you tighten the nuts too much.

Chapter 6

Laundry Rooms

The simplest way to tackle that endless cycle of dirty clothes and linens is to keep your laundry room and appliances in top working condition.

Freshen a clothes washer.

Unless you use your washer every day, it can develop unpleasant odors. There are several things you can do to control odors and keep your washer fresh. First, if you have a top-loading unit, leave the lid open between loads. Second, run the empty washer through a cycle with hot water, detergent and bleach once a month or so.

Level a washer from side to side.

Washers are not meant to walk. If you've ever seen one lumber across a floor during a cycle, you know that while it's entertaining, it's also bad news for the floor and the washer. The key to keeping a washer in place is to keep it level. Put a level on top of the washer and look at the center bubble. It should be centered within the window, between the black lines. If not, you'll need to adjust the washer's front legs. Get an adjustable wrench, and lie down in front of the washer. You'll see that the legs are actually screws that can be turned. Decide whether to raise one side or lower the other. (Try to keep the washer as close to the floor as possible and still level.) Turn the screw clockwise to lower the foot or counterclockwise to raise it. Keep adjusting and checking until the washer is level from side to side.

Level a washer from front to back.

The back of a washer is difficult to reach, so most washers have self-adjusting feet on the back that automatically adjust to the changes you make on the front feet. Even so, you may need to reset them after leveling the front feet. Unplug the washer, and recruit a helper. Grab the back of the washer, and pull it up toward you until the back feet are about 4 inches off the floor. Make sure everything and everyone is out of the way, and then let go of the washer. When the washer drops, the back feet should readjust themselves. Check the washer with a level again, and repeat this process if necessary.

Clean the door gasket on a front-loading washer.

Grime and mildew can build up on the rubber gasket of a front-loading washing machine door. Once a month or so, scrub the gasket with a mild, non-abrasive cleaner such as 409 or Chlorox Cleanup. Rinse thoroughly, and dry the gasket well.

Replace washer hoses.

Water flows into the washer through hoses that connect the water supply pipes to the unit. These flexible rubber hoses are under pressure all the time, even when you're not using the washer. Inspect them every couple of months, checking for cracks or signs of wear. They should flex easily if you bend them gently. If they're brittle, replace them right away before they burst: A burst hose sprays water everywhere and makes a terrible mess. Most hoses are threaded onto the washer as well as the supply lines. Turn off the water supply valves, pull the washer away from the wall, and unplug it. Unscrew the hoses, and take them along to the appliance center, hardware store, or home center to get replacements. If there are inlet screens inside the inlet valves (located on the back of your washer where water flows in), pry them out, and take them along as well. Read and follow manufacturer's instructions on the replacement hoses, but the general idea is that you simply attach them to the connections the same way you took them off.

> **Quick Tip** To avoid potential problems, don't leave the washer running when you leave the house. Turn off the water supply to the washer any time you're going to be away from home for more than a few days.

Check the spin cycle on your washer.

A regular load of laundry should dry in about 40 minutes. If your dryer is working, but it takes a long time to dry one load, the problem may be with the washer rather than with the dryer—the spin cycle may be leaving too much water in the load. To check, fill the washer, and set the dial for the final spin. Let the cycle run for about 90 seconds, then check the tub: All the water should have drained out. If there's still water in the tub, have a repair person adjust the spin cycle.

Clean an electric dryer.

Dryer lint is extremely flammable, so keeping dryer vents clean is critical. At least once a year—once a season if you do lots of laundry—clean the dryer's vent system. Unplug the dryer, or turn off the power to the circuit. Pull the dryer away from the wall, and disconnect the vent hose from the wall vent as well as from the dryer itself. Use the brush attachment on a vacuum cleaner to remove dust and lint from inside the dryer. (You may have to take off the back panel. Check the owner's manual for instructions.) Use the vacuum cleaner or a lamb's wool duster to clean out the vent hose. Replace the hose, put the dryer back in place, and restore power.

Clean a gas dryer.

Sorry, folks. This isn't a job you can do yourselves. Moving a gas dryer can rupture the gas line, which is not something you want to risk. Once a year, schedule a repair person to inspect and clean your dryer.

Clean the dryer vent outlet.

Whether the dryer is gas or electric, you need to check the vent outlet every month or so. Pull out any lint, and make sure the outlet isn't obstructed in any way.

Quick Tip The moisture released by an unvented dryer—almost a gallon of water with every load—encourages mold and mildew to grow. If your dryer isn't vented to the outdoors, get it done right away.

Chapter 7

Systems Made Simple

PLUMBING, ELECTRICITY, AND HVAC

Most of us don't pay much attention to the basic systems of our houses until something goes wrong. If the water stops flowing or the electricity goes out for some reason, we are quick to remember their value. Here are some simple repairs to keep them functioning properly.

Plumbing

Check the temperature of your water supply.

Let the hot water run for four or five minutes, then hold a candy thermometer in the stream for about a minute. Turn off the water, and check the thermometer. If the water is hotter or cooler than 120°, adjust the thermostat on the water heater.

Test the pressure—relief valve on a water heater.

On the side of the thermostat near the top of the water heater, you'll find a brass valve and a lever. This is the pressure-relief valve. Its job is to keep steam from building up inside and rupturing the tank. Once a year, you need to check the valve and make sure it's still working. Lift up on the lever, and let it snap back. A burst of water should come out of the drain pipe below the valve. It not, hire a repair person to replace the valve.

Quick Tip To help protect children from burns, keep the thermostat on your water heaters set to 120°F.

Set the temperature of your hot water.

In most homes, you'll find the water heater near the furnace. A water heater is a large tank, often white or gray, with two water supply lines and an exhaust flue on top. Near the bottom, you'll see a large label, a thermostat, and a dial. Before doing anything else, read the label for other important information. Adjust the water temperature by setting the dial to 120°F. If the dial uses words instead of numbers (e.g., hot, hotter), check the owner's manual to see where to set it. Wait at least an hour, and retest the water temperature (see above).

> **Quick Tip** Make sure you can locate your water supply shutoff valve if a pipe bursts or some other emergency plumbing issue arises. Most are found near the point where the water supply lines enter the house. If the house has a basement, it will usually be there. Find and test the main shutoff valve in your house, and then share this information with every member of your family.

Test shutoff valves. Shutoff valves control the flow of water to individual fixtures, such as sinks, toilets, clothes washers, and ice makers. They're used to shut off the water quickly in case of emergency or when you need to work on a fixture. When these valves get worn out, they can leak. Test shutoff valves for leaks every month or two. To test a shutoff valve, turn the handle back and forth several times. If the valve is leaking or you can't move the handle, call a plumber, and have it checked or replaced right away.

Flush a noisy water heater.

Water heaters gurgle and rumble when sediment builds up in the bottom of the tank. Sediment makes the water heater less efficient and can eventually clog the drain. To remove it, turn off the unit. (If the heater is gas, set the gas valve to "pilot." If it's electric, turn off the power to the circuit.) Connect a hose to the drain valve at the bottom of the tank. Put the other end of the hose in a sink or on a floor drain. Close the valve on the cold-water inlet, and pull up the lever on the pressure-relief valve. Turn on the drain valve, but be careful—the water coming out will

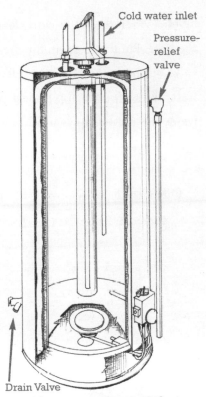

Cold water inlet

Pressure-relief valve

Drain Valve

Inside your water heater: To fix a noisy heater, flush out the sediment that builds at the bottom of the tank.

179

be hot! When the water runs clear, turn off the drain valve and remove the hose. Put the lever on the pressure-relief valve down, and open the valve on the cold-water inlet. Elsewhere in the house, turn on a hot-water faucet (on the top floor if you have more than one) and let the water run until it flows steadily, with no air bubbles. Turn the water heater back on.

Quick Tip If you see water on the floor under a water heater, call a service person immediately. Leaks tell you that the tank is deteriorating. If the tank gives way, there will be a flood of hot water, which can be very dangerous and destructive.

Insulate water pipes.

Insulating water pipes can reduce energy costs, especially if the pipes run through unheated spaces, like crawl spaces. Pick up sleeve-type foam insulation at your local hardware store or home center. These foam tubes are slit lengthwise. All you have to do is open the tube, fit it around the pipe, and press it into shape around the pipe. Close off the hot water supply, and wait for the pipes to cool before insulating them. Be sure to cover at least the first ten feet of the hotwater pipes leaving the water heater and all pipes running through uninsulated spaces.

Quick Tip Pipes that supply sinks on outside walls are especially vulnerable to freezing. Insulating these pipes helps, but during extreme weather, leave the faucet on just enough to drip slowly and open the cabinet doors under the sink so warm air from the room gets into the cabinet and protects the pipes.

Thaw a frozen pipe.

This repair takes a little more than ten minutes, but the problem is common, and the fix is easy, so I'm going to tell you anyway. If the water coming from a faucet turns extremely cold, or no water comes out when you turn on a faucet, grab a flashlight and check the pipes right away. If the pipes are visible, you may find one that's split and leaking. If you don't see any tell-tale signs, follow the pipes to identify the one that supplies the faucet that's not working. Turn off the water at the main shutoff valve, (see page 178), and slowly warm the length of the pipe with a hair dryer or heat gun. (This will take half an hour or so.) Test the faucet. If no water comes out after two or three minutes, reheat the pipe, and try again.

Caution: Electricity and water don't mix. If there's standing water in the area, don't try to thaw the pipe yourself. Turn off the water at the main shutoff valve, and call an emergency plumber. If the frozen pipes run behind finished walls or ceilings, call a plumber—this is *much* more than a ten-minute repair.

Patch a leaky pipe.

As you may remember from high school physics, water expands when it freezes. When water freezes inside a supply pipe, the expansion can produce enough pressure to burst the pipe. Sleeve clamp repair kits are the easiest way to fix the problem until the plumber arrives. These kits, which consist of a rubber sleeve and a two-part clamp, are available at hardware stores and home centers everywhere. Keeping one or two on hand all the time is a good idea, especially if you've had trouble with frozen pipes in the past. Turn off the water at the main shutoff valve and thaw the frozen area (see page 182). Wait until the water has drained from the pipe, then smooth the edges of the split with a metal file. Put the rubber sleeve from the kit over the split, and then cover it with the metal clamps. Firmly tighten the screws that hold the pieces of the clamp together. While these kits are easy to use and work well in an emergency, they provide only a temporary fix. Have a plumber replace this section of pipe as soon as possible.

Fix a leaky sillcock.

Usually a leaky outdoor faucet, or sillcock, just needs a new O-ring or washer (rubber rings that help prevent leaks between connections). Replacement parts are available at any hardware store or home center. Remove the handle and loosen the retaining nut with slip-joint pliers. Remove the stem, and then replace the O-ring on the retaining nut or stem. Unscrew the stem screw, and replace the washer, and then put the assembly back together.

Repair a leaky hose bib.

Hose bibs—faucets with threaded spouts that can be connected to utility or appliance hoses—leak when the washers or seals wear out. You'll find replacements in universal washer kits, available in hardware stores and home centers. First, take a look at the handle on top of the faucet. You'll see a screw in the center of the handle. Loosen and remove that screw, then lift off the handle. Now, you'll see a large packing nut right above the faucet. With the handle off, you'll be able to loosen that nut with an adjustable wrench and remove it along with the packing washer. Next, unscrew and remove the spindle. If you can't turn it by hand, use an adjustable wrench. Cover the jaws of the wrench with masking tape first, being careful not to damage the spindle. Turn the spindle upside down, and remove the stem screw and washer. Coat the new stem washer and packing washer with heat-proof grease, and reverse this process to put the hose bib back together.

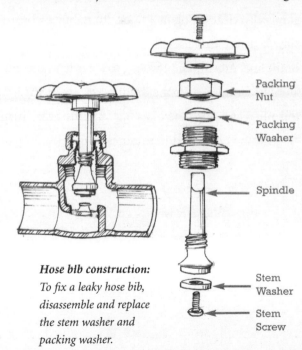

Packing Nut

Packing Washer

Spindle

Stem Washer

Stem Screw

Hose bib construction: *To fix a leaky hose bib, disassemble and replace the stem washer and packing washer.*

Clear a clogged floor drain.

Floor drains usually are located near the furnace and water heater in the mechanical area of most homes or in other areas of the basement or garage. To clear a clog in a floor drain, buy or borrow a blow bag, a simple device that uses water pressure to blow the clog out of the trap or drain line. Attach the blow bag to a garden hose, and connect the hose to a utility faucet. Under the drain cover, you'll see a cleanout plug. Remove this plug, and push the blow bag into the hole. Turn on the water. The clog should be cleared in minutes. If not, it's time to consult a plumber.

Quick Tip Faucet leaks are expensive: A fast drip can waste as much as 429 gallons of water and 107 kilowatt hours every month. To fix a leak, disassemble the faucet and look for the source. Pay attention to how the parts are positioned as you take them apart. If you're nervous about getting it all back together, label the parts and draw diagrams as you go.

Stop spout leaks on a ball faucet.

Beneath the single handle of a ball faucet, a hollow metal or plastic ball controls the temperature and flow of water. If a ball faucet leaks from the spout, grip the knurled edges of the faucet cap with slip-joint pliers, and tighten the cap. If that doesn't stop the leak, turn off the water at the shutoff valves, and take the faucet apart. Use an Allen wrench to loosen the setscrew, then lift off the handle. Grip the faucet cap with your slip-joint pliers, and remove it. Make sure your sink drain is closed before you start taking out the small parts. Next, lift out the cam, cam washer, and ball. With a small screw driver, pry out the springs and the valve

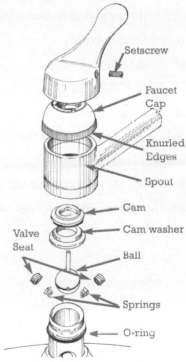

Ball faucet construction: For serious sprout leaks, take a ball faucet apart and replace the parts.

seats. Take these parts to a hardware or home center so you can identify the right replacement parts. Reassemble the faucet with the new parts, and the leak should be gone.

Stop leaks from the base of a ball faucet.
When a ball faucet leaks from the base, you'll need to replace the O-rings. Turn off the shut-off valves, and remove the handle assembly (see page 187). Next, twist the spout up and off to remove it, then cut off the old O-rings. Coat new O-rings with heatproof grease, and put them in place. Press the spout down until its collar settles on the plastic slip ring, then put the handle assembly back together. Turn the faucet on, and gradually open the shutoff valves, watching for leaks. Tighten the connections if necessary.

Stop a leaky cartridge faucet.
If you take the handle off of your faucet and find a cartridge and mov-

able stem, you've got a cartridge faucet. Worn seals are the cause of most spout leaks on these faucets, and the best thing to do is to replace the cartridge. Turn off the water at the shutoff valves, then pry off the index cap, and remove the screw in the center of the faucet handle. Lift the handle up and tilt it backward to get it off. The next thing you'll come to is a plastic retaining ring—use slip-joint pliers to turn it counterclockwise and remove it. If there is a retaining clip holding the cartridge in place, remove it. Now we've come to the good part: grip the cartridge with your slip-joint pliers, and pull straight up. Take the cartridge to the store, and find a replacement. Reverse this process to install the new

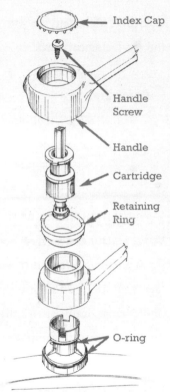

Index Cap

Handle Screw

Handle

Cartridge

Retaining Ring

O-ring

Cartridge faucet construction:
To fix a leaky cartridge faucet, take it apart and replace the cartridge.

cartridge. Make sure the cartridge is lined up just like the old one, with the tab facing forward.

Quick Tip If the hot and cold water are reversed on your cartridge faucet, take it apart again, and rotate the cartridge 180°. Reassemble the faucet, and cold should be cold and hot should be hot.

Stop leaks from the base of a cartridge faucet. Most leaks from a base are caused by worn out O-rings. Disassemble the faucet (see page 189), then pull up and twist the spout to remove it. Cut the old O-rings, and remove them. Coat the new O-rings with heatproof grease, and install them. Reassemble the spout and faucet, then turn the faucet on, and gradually open the shutoff valves. Check for leaks, and tighten connections as necessary.

Stop leaks in a disc faucet.

Disc faucets have a single handle and a wide cylinder inside. Whether they come from the spout or around the body, most leaks are caused by dirty seals or cylinder openings. To fix them, turn off the water at the shutoff valves. Turn the faucet spout to the side, then lift the handle. Remove the setscrew, and lift off the handle and cap. Several screws hold the cylinder in place: remove them and lift out the cylinder. If it looks worn, take it to the store, and buy a new one. If it looks ok, carefully remove the seals from the cylinder openings, then use a scrubbie pad to clean the openings and inlet holes.

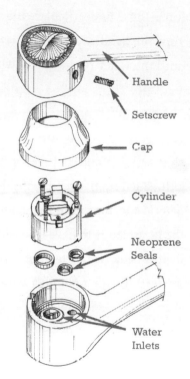

Disc faucet construction: *Take apart a leaky disc faucet to clean inside and replace a worn cylinder.*

Rinse the cylinder. Replace the seals, and put the faucet back together. Turn the handle to ON, and *very* gradually open the shutoff valves until the water runs steadily, with no bursts of air.

Identify compression faucets.

Compression faucets have separate handles for hot and cold water and a threaded stem assembly inside the body. Once these faucets begin to deteriorate, they need frequent repairs. If yours is giving you trouble, the best plan is to have it replaced. The number and placement of holes in your sink will dictate the type of replacement faucet you can choose, so consult with a plumber before choosing one.

Electricity

Get to know your service panel.

What you may call the fuse box or breaker box is referred to by professionals as a *service panel*. Most service panels installed before 1965 use fuses to protect the circuits; most installed after 1965 use circuit breakers. Find your service panel, and spend some time studying it. If your system uses fuses, replace any that show signs of rust (see page 196). If you see rust inside the panel itself, have an electrician check it right away. If your system has breakers, test them. One at a time, turn each breaker off and back on. If you don't feel a distinct click when you press the switch back to the ON position or, if the lever feels loose, have an electrician check it right away.

Quick Tip Fuses are color-coded and labeled with their amperages. Buy a variety of replacement fuses that match the ones on your service panel.

Make a circuit map.

This is going to take more than ten minutes, but it's worth the time. Every electrical repair begins with shutting off the power. A circuit map—a list identifying the devices protected by each fuse or breaker—takes the guesswork out of shutting off the power. If there's already a circuit map inside your service panel, double-check it. If not, make one. Make a numbered list of all the fuses or breakers, and label the fuses or breakers themselves with numbers on pieces of masking tape. Loosen all the fuses (use a fuse puller for cartridge fuses) or flip all the circuit breakers to the OFF position. Turn on all the lights and ceiling fans in the house, and unplug any electronics with stored information like computers and televisions. Turn on one circuit by tightening its fuse or flipping its breaker. Find the area where the lights came on, and check each switch, fixture, appliance or receptacle in the area until you identify all the devices powered by the circuit. Temporarily label the devices with numbered pieces of masking tape, and put them on your numbered list. Continue until you've identified all the devices served by each circuit in the service panel. (This process is much easier if you recruit a helper or two.) When you finish the list, tape it inside the cover of the service panel.

Find a damaged fuse.

To identify a blown fuse when the power goes out, look for one that's brown or black around the edges. If you don't see one that's discolored, look for one with a melted ribbon. If you were using a small appliance, like a toaster or vacuum, when the power went out, check the plug and cord for damage, and repair or replace it as necessary. If the problem persists, have an electrician check the circuit for a short.

Quick Tip Before working on a service panel, put on a pair of sturdy tennis shoes or other rubber-soled shoes as added protection against electrocution.

Replace a plug fuse.

After you've identified the blown plug fuse, check to see what amperage it carries. (Check the color—typically, blue fuses are 15 amps, red or orange or 20, and green are 30. Read the label to double-check.) Unplug or turn off the devices on the circuit, and make sure the floor beneath the service panel is dry. Turn the fuse counterclockwise to remove it. Place a new fuse of the same amperage into the socket, and turn it clockwise.

Locate and restore power to a tripped circuit.

If the lights go out or the outlets stop working in one area of the house, you probably have a tripped circuit. Restoring the power is easy: Open the service panel and look at the breaker levers. The lever on the tripped breaker will be either in the OFF position or in a position between ON and OFF. Press the lever all the way to the OFF position, then press it to the ON position

Replace a cartridge fuse.

If an appliance suddenly loses power, check the cartridge fuses (the long cylindrical fuses) in the service panel. You can't identify blown cartridge fuses by looking at them—you have to test the fuses to find the one that failed. Grab the handle of the fuse block, and pull it out. Don't touch the fuses with your bare hands. Place the head of a fuse puller around the center of the first fuse, and pull. When the fuse is out of the fuse block, test it with a continuity tester. Put the clip on one end and the probe on the other. If the tester lights up, the fuse is working. If not, replace it with a fuse that has the same amperage.

> **Quick Tip** Plug a rechargeable flashlight into an outlet near the main service panel. If a fuse blows or a breaker trips, you'll have plenty of light to find the problem, and you'll always know where to find a working flashlight if the power goes out.

Quick Tip If a circuit breaker trips repeatedly, there may be a problem with the circuit or with the breaker itself. Have an electrician check it.

Test and Reset a Ground-Fault Circuit Interrupter.

A Ground-Fault Circuit Interrupter (GFCI) is a receptacle (a.k.a. outlet) that protects you from electrical shock. A GFCI senses tiny changes in current and can shut off the power in as little as 1/40th of a second if necessary. Most local building codes now require them in bathrooms, kitchens, garages, crawl spaces, unfinished basements, and outdoor receptacle locations. To test a GFCI, press the TEST button. Plug a lamp or hair dryer into the receptacle. It shouldn't work. Next, press the RESET button. The lamp should light up, or the hairdryer should turn on. If a GFCI fails this test, consult an electrician.

Test a switch for power.

If you're going to do any work at all on your electrical system, you need a *circuit tester*, an inexpensive device available at hardware stores and home centers everywhere. With a circuit tester, you can be sure the power is off and that it's safe to work on the system. Remove the switch cover plate and mounting screws, and carefully pull the switch out of the box. Hold onto the mounting straps (the little "ears" on the top and bottom of the switch) only, and don't touch any bare wires or screw terminals until you've tested for power. If the switch box is metal and has a grounding screw, touch one of the circuit tester's probes to the box and the other to one screw terminal and then the other. The tester shouldn't light up at all. If the switch box is plastic, put one probe on the bare copper (grounding) wire, and touch the other to one screw terminal and then the other. Again, the tester shouldn't light up at all. If it does, go back to the service panel, and turn off the right circuit. Repeat the test until you're sure the power to the circuit is off.

Shut off the power to a circuit.

This is the time when a circuit map comes in handy (see page 194). If you've already made one, congratulations! If not, what are you waiting for? Identify the proper circuit and remove the fuse or flip the circuit breaker to the OFF position. Plug in a lamp or small appliance and turn it on. If nothing happens, you can be sure that the power is off.

Test a receptacle for power. Insert one of the probes of a circuit tester into each of the outlet's slots. If the tester lights, the receptacle is receiving power. Go back to the service panel, and try again. Repeat the test. When the tester does not light, you're ready for the next step. Take off the cover plate, and pull the receptacle from the box. (Be careful not to touch any of the wires until you've confirmed that the power to the circuit is off.) Touch one probe of the circuit tester to the brass screw terminal and the other to the silver screw terminal. If there are wires connected to both sets of terminals, test both sets. If the tester lights up at any time during this test, power is reaching the receptacle. Go back to the service panel, and turn off the right circuit.

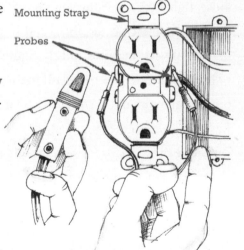

Mounting Strap

Probes

Check an outlet for power: *Touch the probes of a circuit tester to the screw terminals to test for power.*

Repair a receptacle.

Receptacles hardly ever go bad, but it can happen. Before you do anything else, turn off the power to the circuit and test the receptacle for power (see page 201). When you've confirmed that the power is off, check out the wires on the screw terminals. If the connections are loose, tighten them. If the wires are nicked, darkened, or dirty, remove them from the screw terminals and rub the ends with fine-grit sandpaper. Reconnect the wires and check the connections. (Be careful not to tighten the screws too much.) If there's dust or dirt in the receptacle box, clean it out and then replace the receptacle and cover plate. Restore power to the circuit and test the receptacle. If it doesn't work, check the other receptacles on the circuit. If they're working, have an electrician replace the receptacle.

Strip electrical wires.

Electrical wire is protected by a nonconductive plastic or rubber sheathing. Before you can connect the wire to any device, you need to remove this coating. To do this, you need a combination tool, a tool that looks like a pair of pliers with a series of notches on the inside edges. Look for the marks designating the gauge of wire you're using, and clamp that notch around the wire. Firmly slide the tool toward the end to separate the insulation from the wire.

Connect electrical wire to a screw terminal.

To repair or replace a receptacle or switch, you have to connect wires to the screw terminals on the device. This can be frustrating if you don't know how, but it's a breeze if you do it right. Strip about ¾ of an inch of insulation from the end of the wire. Grip the stripped wire with needle nose pliers and form it into a C-shaped loop. Hook the wire around the screw terminal so the loop is turning clockwise and the insulation is just touching the head of the screw. Tighten the screw.

Quick Tip If a switch plates gets hot, or you can hear a buzzing noise coming from the switch, a loose wire may be touching the side of the metal box. This is dangerous. Turn off power to the circuit immediately. If you're confident of your skills, you can fix this yourself easily enough. If you're not sure, call an electrician right away.

Fix a switch by tightening a loose wire. Turn off power to the circuit, and test to confirm that the power is off (see page 199). Look inside the box for the loose wire and check it for damage. If it's darkened or nicked, clean the end with fine-grit sandpaper. Hook the end of the wire around the screw terminal, and tighten the screw. Restore power to the circuit, and carefully test the switch to make sure it still works. If it does, carefully place the switch back in the box, and put on the cover plate.

Connect wires using a wire connector. Read the chart on the package to find the gauge and number of wires the connector can hold. To connect wires using this tool, strip about half an inch of insulation from each wire. Hold the wires together, and clip them so that the ends are even and the stripped portions are the same length. Still holding the wires together, push them into the wire connector, and turn it clockwise until it feels snug. Gently pull the wire to make sure the connection is tight, and check to make sure you can't see any bare wire outside the connector. If you can, take off the connector, trim the ends of the wire, and replace the connector.

Wire Connector

Using a wire connecter:
Push the ends of the stropped
wires into the connector and
turn clockwise.

Wires

Replace a worn lamp cord.

If a frisky puppy decides a lamp cord is a chew toy, don't throw the lamp—or the puppy—out. Don't pay an electrician a small fortune to fix the lamp, either. Buy a new lamp cord at a hardware store or home center, and rewire it. You'll be surprised how much confidence you'll build once you realize that you can rewire a lamp. It might lead you to perform all sorts of wiring projects! Start by unplugging the lamp and removing the lampshade. Take a look at the illustration provided here, and identify the parts, then use the screwdriver to loosen the terminal screws and remove the old wires. Pull the cord down through the lamp base, and throw it away. Thread

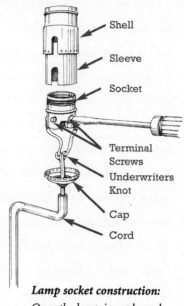

Lamp socket construction: Once the lamp is unplugged, loosen the terminal screws, as shown, to rewire a lamp.

the new cord through the base and up through the stem to the socket cap. Most replacement lamp cords are pre-split and the ends are stripped to make it easier to wire the lamp. (If the one you bought isn't prepared this way, use a knife to split the last 2 inches of the cord along the midline of the insulation. Strip ½ to ¾ of an inch of insulation from the end of each of the wires.) Now, you're ready to tie your first underwriter's knot. Form an overhand loop with one wire and an underhand loop with the other. Slide the end of each wire through the loop of the other. The resulting knot will look a lot like a pretzel. Make a C-loop on the end of each wire (see page 203), then look carefully at each. On one wire the insulation is rounded, and on the other it has a fine line or ribs. Connect the rounded wire to the brass screw and the ribbed wire to the silver screw. Tighten the terminal screws. Adjust the underwriter's knot to fit within the socket cap, then position the socket in the socket cap. Slide the insulating sleeve and outer shell over the socket so the terminal screws are completely covered. Put in a light bulb, and test the lamp. If it works, press the socket cover into the socket cap until it locks in place. If not, check your work, especially the connections at the terminal screws.

Fix a lamp by adjusting the tab in the lamp socket.

Sometimes a lamp doesn't work for what seems like no reason at all. You've changed the light bulb, tested the outlet, and rechecked the connections on the terminal screws. Everything's fine, and yet the lamp doesn't work. This is when a little knowledge of electricity's eccentricities comes in handy: Electricity, like karma, travels in a circle. Translation: The metal tab at the bottom of the socket has to touch the bottom of the light bulb in order for current to reach the bulb. To solve the problem, unplug the lamp. (Let me repeat that: *Unplug the lamp.*) Remove the light bulb, and look into the socket. Use a screwdriver to pry up the little metal tab at the bottom of the socket. Put the bulb back in, and it's an odds-on bet that the lamp will work.

Quick Tip Investing in wire connectors will make most electrical projects easier. Keep a supply of sizes on hand. You can find them in the electrical department of a hardware store or home center.

Replace a fluorescent tube. Fluorescent tubes last a long time—about three years, typically. Eventually though, they start flickering or light only partially, and it's time to replace them. Turn off the circuit to the fixture, and test to confirm that the power is off. Remove the cover, if there is one, then turn the tube toward you about a quarter of a turn, and slide it out of the sockets. Carefully set the old tube aside. Put the new tube in place, slide the pins all the way into the sockets, and twist the tube about a quarter of a turn.

Quick Tip Don't put fluorescent tubes into the trash because they contain mercury. If you don't know where to take them, call your local hazardous waste disposal site for advice.

Remove a broken light bulb.

When a light bulb breaks off in the socket, it's a challenge to remove but not a problem. First, unplug the lamp, or turn off the power to the circuit. Next, press a bar of soap into the broken glass until it's secure. Turn the soap like a handle to remove the bulb. (If you don't have a bar of soap in the house, try a raw potato. It should work just as well.)

Clean chandelier crystals.

You can buy sprays that clean chandelier crystals, but they're fairly expensive, and the process is messy. My favorite way of cleaning chandelier crystals is much less expensive and a good deal easier. Pour ¼ cup of ammonia and ¾ of a cup of white vinegar into a small jar. Cover the floor under the chandelier with a drop cloth or clean newsprint. Hold the jar below the chandelier, dip a crystal into the solution, and let it drip into the jar for a moment. Continue until you've dipped all the crystals, then stand back, and admire your work.

Clean a cloth lampshade.

Cloth lampshades can't be washed, but they can be cleaned. Combine ½ a cup of liquid dish soap, 1/2 a teaspoon of ammonia, 1 teaspoon of white vinegar, and 1 quart of warm water. Mix the solution with an electric mixer or hand whisk to produce a thick layer of foam. Scoop up some of the foam with a sponge, and blot it onto the shade. Wipe off the foam with a clean, damp cloth, and dry the clean shade with a hair dryer on a cool setting.

Heating, Ventilation, and Air Conditioning

Test your smoke detectors.

Smoke detectors save lives, but only if they work. Test them every month and after any extended absence. Press the TEST button for five to ten seconds, and then release it. If the alarm sounds, press the RESET button. If not, replace the batteries. If that doesn't solve the problem, check the wire connections. If the connections are secure, and the detector still isn't working, have an electrician replace it.

Inspect and change a standard furnace filter.

Dirty filters reduce the efficiency of the furnace and circulate dust and dirt through your house, so inspect the filters in your furnace once a month. Find the filter compartment (check the owner's manual for the precise location), and remove the access cover. Carefully slide the filter out of its compartment, and hold it up to a light. If the light doesn't shine through it, replace the filter with a new one.

Change the batteries in a smoke detector. It may surprise you to hear that even hard-wired smoke detectors have batteries. (They back up the system when the power fails.) It's critical to change the batteries in your smoke detectors as soon as they beep to signal that the battery is low. In addition, change the batteries once a year. Choose a date that's easy to remember—your birthday or the end of daylight savings time in the fall, for example. Remove the cover, and locate the battery. Remove the old battery, and install the new one. Before replacing the cover, vacuum it to remove dust and dirt (dust and dirt reduce the sensor's ability to detect smoke).

Clean an electrostatic filter. An electrostatic filter, an appliance designed to further clean the air circulating through the furnace, is attached to the furnace. To clean this system, turn off the system, then remove the access cover, and pull the filters from the unit. Wash the filters with cool water and a soft scrub brush, or run them through the "Light" cycle (but not the "Dry" cycle) in the dishwasher. Let the filters air dry, then but them back in place and turn on the system again.

Quick Tip If your home was built before the late 1970s, identify the materials that contain asbestos, and make sure they are not disturbed. Touching or handling asbestos may release microscopic particles into the air that can cause skin irritations or respiratory problems, including lung cancer. If materials in your home containing asbestos are damaged or need to be removed for some reason, contact an asbestos abatement specialist.

Check vent pipes. Gas forced-air furnaces produce exhaust fumes, which are carried out of the house through vent pipes. Unfortunately, the condensation produced by a furnace is very acidic and can corrode these metal pipes. Corroded vent pipes need to be replaced *immediately,* because they leak carbon monoxide, a very dangerous gas. At the beginning and end of every heating season, inspect the vent pipes for signs of corrosion. If you see anything suspicious, call an HVAC specialist or your natural gas provider.

> **Quick Tip** Carbon monoxide is invisible and has no smell. Have your
> furnace, chimneys, wood stoves or fireplaces, exhaust flues, and all
> oil or gas appliances inspected once a year and install carbon
> monoxide detectors in your home. Place a detector at least 15 feet
> away from the furnace or water heater, and another in the bedroom
> hallway. If your house has more than one level, place a detector on
> each level.

Maintain carbon monoxide detectors. Test and clean your
carbon monoxide detectors every month, and replace the batteries
once a year. Vacuum the cover, and then press the TEST button for 5 to
10 seconds. The alarm should sound. If not, replace the batteries. If the
alarm is hardwired, check the circuit breaker or fuse, too. If the alarm
still doesn't work, replace it.

Clean the air intake and exhaust. If you have a forced air furnace, there is an air intake and an exhaust somewhere outside your house. Both these tubes need access to fresh air at all times for the furnace to operate safely and efficiently. Every month or so, check these areas to make sure they're not blocked by plants, bushes, snow, spider webs, or debris. Clear them if necessary.

Clean a baseboard heater. Dirty baseboard heaters don't keep a room as warm as clean ones do. To clean a baseboard heater, turn off the power, and use a circuit tester to make sure the power is off. Remove the front panel, and use the crevice tool on a vacuum cleaner to remove dust and dirt from the element. If any of the fins are badly bent, use a pair of needle nose pliers to straighten them. (Don't worry about slightly bent fins—they don't hurt anything.) Replace the cover, and restore the power.

Clean a radiator.

A clean radiator is an efficient radiator, so clean yours at least once a month. Close the valve, and let the radiator cool, then use the brush tool on your vacuum cleaner to dust the surface of the radiator and a lamb's wool duster to clean between the fins. After dusting, wash the radiator with warm water and a little detergent.

Inspect a wood-burning fireplace.

Before you build the first fire of the season, inspect the damper, flue, and firebox. This is easy but messy, so wear a hat and old clothes. Open the damper, and use an old toilet brush to clean around its edges. With a wet/dry vac, vacuum the soot from the firebox, and then stick your head inside and look up—you should see light at the top of the flue. If you can't fit far enough into the firebox to see, use a flashlight and a mirror. If you can't see light, the flue may be blocked. Don't build a fire when the flue is blocked until a chimney sweep has inspected the fireplace. If the flue is clear, make sure the damper closes tightly. If you're not sure, contact a chimney sweep.

Quick Tip According to the Consumer Product Safety Commission, in a recent year more than 15,000 house fires started in chimneys and fireplaces. Have your chimney cleaned by a professional at least once a year.

Adjust the flames in a gas fireplace.

The flames in a gas fireplace should be blue with yellowish tips. If the flames in your fireplace don't look like that, adjust the primary air shutter, which you should find on the control panel. If that doesn't fix the problem, call a fireplace specialist.

Paint a radiator.

If a painted radiator looks shabby, or you're redecorating, it's time to repaint. Before you start, close the valve, and let the radiator cool for 24 hours. Sand the radiator with fine-grit sandpaper, and wipe away the dust. Prime any bare areas with a metal primer, and let the primer dry. Paint retailers offer special radiator paint, but most latex paints will work just fine. (Many paint retailers also offer a flexible paint tool made especially for painting radiators; this tool is worth the money.) Paint the areas between the fins first, then work your way to the main surfaces. Let the paint dry completely before opening the valve to restore the heat. Don't worry if you smell paint when the radiator heats up. This is normal and will go away in time.

Quick Tip To increase the amount of heat a radiator puts out, paint it a dark color, and then place a piece of aluminum or sheet metal behind it.

Balance a ceiling fan.

Ceiling fans wobble when a blade is loose or out of alignment. To get rid of the wobble, tighten all the screws that hold the blades to the brackets and the brackets to the fixture. If that doesn't solve the problem, measure the distance from the ceiling to the same point on each blade. If they're not all the same distance, gently bend the blade brackets as necessary to get the blades aligned. If the fan still wobbles, buy a blade balancing kit at a hardware store or home center, and follow the instructions.

> **Quick Tip** Before working on a ceiling fan when other people are around, turn off the switches and crisscross masking tape over them. Post a note if the fan can't be seen from the switch location. You don't want someone to walk into the room and hit the switch without thinking while your head is in the path of the fan blades.

Clean the filter in an air-to-air exchanger.

Air-to-air exchangers are the HVAC industry's answer to the lack of fresh air in today's super-insulated homes. Most new homes have an exchanger-in some communities, building codes even require them. If you have one, you'll find it near the furnace. One large duct runs from the exchanger, housed in a metal box, to an outside wall; another one runs to the furnace. Like most air-handling equipment, they have filters that need to be cleaned periodically. Depending on the manufacturer's recommendations, clean the air filter every one to three months. Remove the cover, and take out washable filters; clean them with mild soap and water. Let the filters dry completely before you put them back. Replace disposable filters.

Clean the heat recovery core on an air-to-air exchanger.

A heat recovery core transfers heat from indoor air to the fresh air coming into the heating system. Because it handles outdoor air, the recovery core has filters that clean the incoming air. To clean the core, remove the cover of the exchanger, and slide out the metal rods that hold the core in place. Clean the core with cool water and mild detergent, then rinse it thoroughly. Let the core dry thoroughly before you replace it.

Reverse a ceiling fan for changes in weather.

Turn the fan on, and watch which direction the blades turn. They should go clockwise in cold weather and counterclockwise in warm. If the rotation doesn't match the season, turn the fan off and get out a stepladder. Check out the head at the center of the fan—you're looking for a sliding switch. If you find one, slide the switch in the opposite direction, and then move yourself and the ladder out of the way. Turn the fan on, and make sure it's turning in the right direction.

Maintain a room air conditioner.

Unplug the unit, and remove the access cover on the front of the unit. Pull out the filter, and wash it with water and a mild detergent. Let the filter dry thoroughly before you put it back. Remove the back panel and vacuum the condenser fins using the brush tool on a vacuum cleaner. Use a fin comb to straighten any bent fins, then replace the back cover. Now look at the back of the unit—you should find a drain hole and a drain pan just below the condenser coils. Soak up any water in the pan with a sponge or rag; inspect and clean the drain hole. Wash the drain pan with equal parts of bleach and water. When you're finished, reinstall the unit.

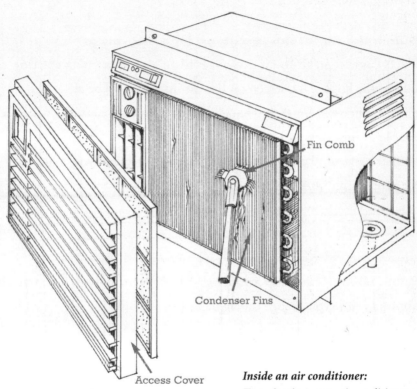

Fin Comb

Condenser Fins

Access Cover

Inside an air conditioner:
*To maintain a room air conditioner,
keep the filter clean and vacuum and
comb the condenser fins.*

Check the air intake screen on an air-to-air exchanger.

Ducts connect an air-to-air exchanger to an air intake on an exterior wall of the house. The screen on this air intake has to be clean and free of debris in order for the exchanger to get fresh air. Check the screen a couple of times a year, and make sure it's not clogged by dirt, debris, animal nests, or plants. In the winter, check it frequently to make sure the screen isn't frozen over.

Clean the condenser tray in an air-to-air exchanger.

Some exchangers include a condenser tray. If your unit has one, wash it out every time you change the filters.

Maintain the condenser unit on a central air conditioner.

The condenser unit is the part of a central air conditioner that's outside. It needs to be clean to work efficiently. Shut off the power at the unit's disconnect switch and at the main service panel. When you're sure the power is off, remove the access panels. Put on some heavy gloves, and remove any debris from around the condenser coil, fan, and motor. Use a garden hose and a soft-bristle brush to wash the outer fins and coils. A fin comb is a tool used to straighten bent fins on a condensing unit. Most fin combs include teeth for several sizes of fins—select the right size, and draw the comb along the fins to straighten any bent ones. Turn the fan and watch whether it rotates smoothly. If not, tighten the screws holding the blades to the brackets. If a blade is bent, have a professional replace the fan assembly.

Quick Tip When it comes to air conditioners, leave anything that involves the capacitor (a high-voltage device that stores an electrical charge) or refrigerant (the gas inside the coils) to the professionals.

Level a central air conditioner's condensing unit.

The condensing unit (the part of a central air conditioner that's outside) has to be level for the air conditioner to work correctly (that's why it sits on a concrete slab). Every spring, check the unit with a level in both directions. The bubble in the center of the level should be centered between the marks. If not, adjust the feet or place thin wood shims under them until the unit is level. If you can't adjust it enough this way, you may have to have a concrete professional repair or replace the slab.

Chapter 8

The Great Outdoors

Most exterior repairs are small and simple but vital to the well-being of the structure of the house. If you can spare just ten minutes here and there, you can keep the exterior of your home in top condition.

Caulk exterior openings.

There are all kinds of openings in the exterior walls of our houses—openings for the water supply, electricity, phone and data lines, sillcocks, and dryer vents, for example. The edges of these openings are filled with flexible caulk. When it fails, moisture, insects, and yes, even rodents, have access to the house. Inspect the openings every spring and fall. If the caulk has shrunk or cracked, clean it out with a utility knife or small screwdriver. Refill the openings with butyl caulk or expandable foam.

Put away the garden hoses for winter.

The water in a garden hose will freeze and split the hose if you leave it outside over a cold winter. Before the first freeze of the season, take the hose off the spigot, and drain it. (I usually do this after I've cleaned the gutters and have the ladder out anyway.) Put one end of the hose at the top of a ladder, and let the rest trail down. After half an hour or so, coil the hose, and store it in the garage or basement for the winter.

Give your front door and entry a bath.

Once a year, power wash your front entry or wash it with a long-handled brush, warm water, and a mild detergent. If you're using a power washer, direct the spray at an angle, and try not to aim the spray at joints of any sort, including mortar joints. Be sure to wash below the eaves and under porches.

Quick Tip Power washers produce some serious water pressure, so test the spray before directing it at the house, and don't aim the nozzle at yourself or anyone else.

Close down the outdoor spigots.

When you put away the garden hoses in the fall, get the sillcock ready for cold weather, too. Find the shutoff valve inside the house, and turn off the water. Turn on the sillcock so any trapped water drains away.

Open a garage door when the automatic opener isn't working.

OK, the electricity's out, or the door opener just died, and you absolutely have to go somewhere. Relax—this is no problem. Take a flashlight out to the garage, and look up at the track, just above the garage door. You should see a handle—often a bright color like red—hanging from a cord. Pull the handle to disengage the opener, and then pull the door up. If all goes well, you're free! If you can't raise the door, the main spring may be broken. This is not something you can fix yourself—call a garage door repair person for help.

Clean brick siding.

Most dirt and stains on brick can be removed with a stiff-bristled brush and water. If that doesn't work, add a little laundry detergent to the water. Rinse the area thoroughly.

Remove smoke stains from bricks.

Dissolve trisodium phosphate (TSP) in water. Use the solution and a scrub brush to clean the brick. Rinse thoroughly.

Weatherstrip a garage door.

The weatherstripping on the bottom of a garage door keeps out rain, snow, dirt, and critters. If it's torn or crumbling, it can't do its job. Rolls of replacement weatherstripping are usually displayed with other door hardware in hardware and home centers. Release the door by pulling on the release cord (see page 232). Open the door until the bottom is within comfortable reach. Pry off the old weatherstripping, and remove the nails. Line up the new piece, and nail it in place. When you reach the edge, trim the weatherstripping to fit the width of the door.

Fix the lock on a garage door. Most garage doors go up and down many times every day, so it's not surprising that the screws and bolts can work loose over time. When that happens, the lock bar can shift out of alignment and the lock won't work correctly. Grab a cup of coffee and a ratchet wrench—you can fix this before the coffee cools. From inside the garage, lower the door, and check out the hinge screws and bolts (see Figure A), on the sides of the door. Use the ratchet wrench to tighten any loose hinge screws or bolts and then replace any missing, broken, or bent hardware. Next, loosen the mounting screws or bolts on the lock. Adjust the lock so the lock bar lines up with the lock hole in the door track. Tighten the screws or bolts (see Figure B), and you're done. Enjoy your coffee.

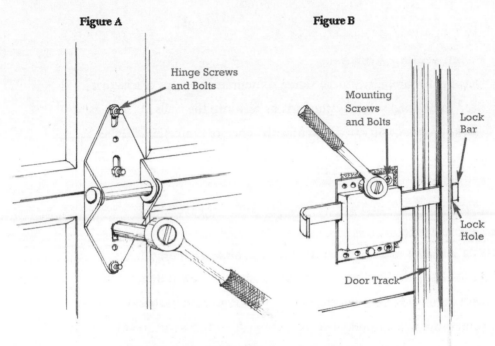

Figure A

Hinge Screws and Bolts

Figure B

Mounting Screws and Bolts

Lock Bar

Lock Hole

Door Track

Fix a garage door lock: *Tighten any loose screw or bolts on the door with a ratchet wrench, as shown in Figure A. Next, loosen the mounting screws or bolts on the lock until the lock bar lines up with the lock hole (Figure B).*

Patch stucco siding.

Despite its durability, stucco siding sometimes develops cracks that need to be filled before water finds its way into the walls. As long as the cracks are thin, you can fill them with concrete caulk. Overfill the crack, then smooth it out with the help of some denatured alcohol and a disposable paint brush.

Fill small holes or dents in aluminum siding.

Instead of patching small areas of damage with new siding, fill them with auto-body filler, which you can find at an auto parts store. I use something called Bondo, two-part epoxy filler that's remarkably easy to shape and sand. You should also be able to find some auto-body paint to help blend the repair into the surrounding siding.

Age cedar shingles for patches.

The color of new cedar shingles makes repairs stick out like a sore thumb unless you age the shingles before putting them in place. Dissolve a cup or so of baking soda in a gallon of water, and brush it onto the new shingles. Let them sit in the sun until their color matches the siding.

Quick Tip Wasps and bees sometimes build nests in the eaves of a house. If you spray wasp or bee killer to eliminate them, avoid the vinyl siding as much as possible. Petroleum-based pesticide products discolor vinyl siding.

Seal a leaky downspout.

The connection between a gutter and a downspout is prone to leaks. If you spot a leak, clean the area thoroughly, and run a bead of rubber-based gutter caulk around the seam at the edges of the downspout.

Reset brick pavers.

The clay paving bricks that make up your courtyard, terrace, walkway, or driveway will need to be reset from time to time. Sand-set pavers sometimes heave after a severe winter or a wet spring. This is easy to fix—all it takes is some sand and patience. Pry up the pavers that aren't level and a few more around them. Rake the sand beneath; add or remove sand if necessary to get the area level. Slowly water the sand, and tamp it down firmly. Put the pavers back in place, and tap them with a rubber mallet to set them. Check the area with a level, and make any adjustments necessary. When the area is level, spread a layer of sand over it, and sweep the sand into the joints. Set up a sprinkler to water the area slowly but thoroughly. Add more sand if necessary to fill the joints.

Clean out a gutter.

Clogged gutters often dump water right down the foundation walls, which leads to water problems of all sorts. When the gutters are full, scoop out the debris with a garden trowel, and flush out the downspouts with the hose. Put the hose down the opening, and stuff a rag around it to direct water down the spout. Turn on the water, and watch what comes out the end: When the clog bursts out, you're done.

> **Quick Tip** If the house has asphalt shingles, and the gutters are filled with granules, have your roof inspected. This is a sign that the shingles are nearing the end of their useful life.

Patch damaged asphalt driveways.

When water finds its way under holes and large cracks in asphalt, it can wash out the gravel base and, eventually, ruin the driveway. Fill holes as soon as you notice them. Vacuum out the hole with a wet/dry vac, and then flush it with a garden hose. Fill the hole with asphalt patching material (available at home centers), mounding it slightly. Warm the area with a heat gun, and then tamp the material with a brick (or some other heavy object) until the patch is level with the surrounding area.

Quick Tip The first time I reset some pavers, I just pulled them out willy-nilly. It was a curved sidewalk set in a herringbone pattern, so it took forever to get the pieces back in the right places. Learn from my mistake: Set the pavers aside in the right order.

Glossary

Alkyd paint: oil-based paint.

Allen wrench: an L-shaped tool with hexagonal ends that fits into a socket in the head of a screw or bolt.

Cartridge fuse: cylindrical fuses that control the 240-volt circuits used by major appliances. They can range from 30 to 100 amps.

Casement window: a window with a vertical sash that's hinged on one side and operated by a crank.

Caulk: a waterproof, flexible substance used to seal joints.

Circuit breaker: a switch that automatically interrupts an electric circuit if the devices on the circuit draw more power than the circuit can safely carry.

Circuit tester: a device used to test for live electrical current.

Circular saw: a power saw with a circular cutting blade.

Condenser unit: the part of an air conditioning or heat pump system where refrigerant is condensed to a liquid state, causing it to cool as it releases heat to the air.

Construction adhesive: heavy-duty adhesive sometimes used to attach lumber to masonry or other surfaces.

Continuity tester: a device that checks for the interrupted flow of electricity within a circuit or appliance.

Countersink: to set the head of a screw or nail at or below the surface.

Damper: a device in a forced-air or hot-water heating system used to control the flow of air or water to various parts of the system. Also: a plate in a fireplace flue used to regulate the draft.

Deadbolt: long bolt that extends into a door jamb. Part of a security lock that is operated by a keyed mechanism.

Denatured alcohol: a form of alcohol, unfit to drink, often used as a solvent.

Doorjamb: the vertical piece that forms the side of a doorway.

Double-hung window: a window that has two sashes that move up and down, one behind the other, along tracks in the opening.

Dowel: a round wood rod or stick often used to hold two pieces of wood together without slipping.

Downspout: a vertical pipe that carries water from the gutter system to the ground.

Drywall screws: screws designed to hold drywall to wall studs. These screws are easy to drive and their bugle-shaped heads let you countersink them in drywall without damaging the surface.

Ducts: a pipe, tube, or channel that carries air or water throughout a system.

Eaves: the lower border of a roof. Eaves hang over the exterior walls.

Exhaust flue: a pipe that directs gases out of the house. For example, the flue on a water heater safely routes carbon monoxide and other gases away from the area of combustion and to the outdoors.

Expandable foam: a product used to fill cracks and holes in exterior especially walls.

Furring strips: narrow pieces of lumber attached to a solid surface to create a flat or level surface for the finish surface. For example, drywall often is screwed to furring strips attached to block or cement walls in finished basements.

Fuse: a safety device that interrupts an electrical circuit if the current exceeds a predetermined amperage.

Graphite powder: a soft, black form of carbon sometimes used as a lubricant.

Grout: a cement product used to fill the crevices between ceramic or stone tile.

Hinge pin: the bolt-like pin that holds the barrels of the hinge together.

Hollow wall anchors: devices designed to support screws in drywall. Used when hanging a picture or other heavy objects in a location that's between wall studs.

Hose bib: a faucet with a threaded spout. Often used to connect utility or appliance hoses to the water supply.

Joist: a horizontal beam that supports a floor or ceiling.

Latch bolt: operating in conjunction with the doorknob, this part extends beyond the side of the door to hold the door closed.

Level: a tool that helps you establish an exactly horizontal line or plane.

O-ring: a ring, usually rubber, used to prevent leaks.

Oxalic acid crystals: an acid ($(COOH)_2$ or H_2C_2O) used as a bleaching or cleaning agent.

Paint stripper: a chemical that removes paint from wood and other surfaces.

Painter's tape: special, easy-release tape used to mask or protect surfaces while you paint.

Plug fuse: a screw-in fuse that controls a 120-volt circuit that provides power for lights and outlets. Plug fuses are rated for 15, 20, or 30 amps.

Popcorn ceiling: a popular type of ceiling texture; looks somewhat like cottage cheese.

Pressure-relief valve: a device that protects the tank of a water heater from being ruptured by the build up of steam.

Prime: to apply a base coat of primer paint in preparation for painting.

Primer: a paint product designed to bond well to any surface and provide a durable base that will keep the paint from cracking or peeling.

Ratchet wrench: a tool used to tighten or loosen bolts and nuts. Includes interchangeable sockets that fit a wide variety of sizes of nuts and bolts.

Receptacle: an electrical outlet.

Ring-shank nails: nails with rings, or threads, built into the body of the nail. These nails are designed to hold heavy materials securely.

Riser: the vertical boards between stairs.

Sash: the frame that surrounds the glass part of a window.

Score: to make a small cut or scratch, using a sharp instrument, to make it easier to cut or break some material. For example, scoring a ceramic tile before snapping it creates a cleaner cut.

Screw extractor: a tool used to remove a stripped screw.

Screw terminals: screws on an electrical switch or outlet to which the circuit wires are connected.

Service panel: a panel of fuses or circuit breakers through which electricity is directed to various household circuits.

Setscrew: a screw that goes through one part and into another to hold the second part in place. For example, the mounting piece on many towel bars have setscrews that hold the bar in place.

Sillcock: a faucet attached to the outside of a house or building.

Solid-surface material: the generic term for a material made from acrylic or polyester resins mixed with additives. Brand names include Corian and Silestone.

Slip-joint pliers: heavy-duty pliers with an adjustable pivot joint that lets them grip objects of varying thicknesses. Sometimes referred to as "channel-lock" pliers.

Spackle: a filler for cracks and holes in wall surfaces.

Storm door: an additional door placed outside an exterior door to provide another layer of protection against severe weather.

Strike plate: the part on the doorjamb into which a latch bolt fits in order to open and close a door.

Stringer: the part of a staircase that extends diagonally from one story to the other to support the stair treads and risers.

Stud: the vertical boards in the framing of a wall. Usually 2 x 4s spaced 16 inches apart.

Subfloor: plywood or cementboard attached to the floor joists to form a foundation for the floor coverings, such as carpet, sheet vinyl, or ceramic tile.

Thermostat: a device that regulates temperature. For example, the thermostat on a water heater senses the temperature of the water in the tank and turns on the heater when necessary to keep the water at an established temperature.

Threshold: the plank, stone, or piece of lumber that lies on the floor under a door.

Trap: the curved section of pipe below a drain. A trap holds standing water to keep sewer gas from rising through the drain and into the house.

Tread: The horizontal platform of the stair—the part you step on.

Trisodium phosphate: a multi-purpose cleaner capable of removing grease and dirt, especially in preparation for new paint.

Weatherstripping: material that covers the edges of a door or window to prevent drafts and keep out rain or snow.

Wind chain: a device that keeps a storm door from opening beyond the reach of its hinges.

Wire connector: a plastic device used to connect two or more electrical wires. Sometimes referred to as "wire caps."

Wood-patching compound: materials used to fill holes in wood. Some can be purchased in colors to match various types of wood; others can be tinted with wood stain.

About the Author

Jerri Farris is the author of *Home Improvement 101*,
IdeaWise Bathrooms, IdeaWise Kitchens, IdeaWise Porches,
and dozens of other books on home improvement and home décor.
Her son is in the Navy, her daughter is in college,
and she now lives in Independence. (Missouri, that is.)

Also from Fair Winds Press

10-Minute Housekeeping
by Rose R. Kennedy
1-59233-177-7
$12.00/£6.99/$17.00 CAN
Available wherever books are sold.

Divide and Conquer Your Mess in No Time at All!

Maintaining a clean house may seem like an overwhelming task, but it doesn't
have to be. Inside, you'll discover a new approach to keeping your home orderly:
by breaking your cleaning time into more manageable, ten-minute segments,
your house will go from grimy to gleaming, and you'll always stay on top of
chores. Packed with hundreds of clever and useful tips, you'll make the most of
what little time you have.

Check out these time-saving gems:

- Grab a sheet of fabric softener to dust off the television.
- Lift tough stains on toys and furniture with a little cream of tartar.
- Switch to natural soap to avoid soap scum build-up and reduce
  scrubbing time
- Squeeze a blob toothpaste on scuff marks and wipe your hardwood floors
  clean
- Soak new plastic shower curtains in warm salted water to prevent mildew
- Burn a CD that groups songs into ten-minute sets for cleaning